BLUE-RINSE
AND
BANOFFEE PIE

Blue-Rinse and Banoffee Pie

RON FERGUSON

Northern Books
from Famedram

From the same author:

Hitler was a Vegetarian

Donald Dewar ate my Hamster

Fear and loathing in Lochgelly

Black Diamonds and the Blue Brazil

Geoff: the Life of Geoffrey M Shaw

ISBN 0905489 81 0
© Copyright 2005 Ron Ferguson and *The Herald*

Published by Famedram Publishers Ltd AB41 9EA
www.northernbooks.co.uk

Printed by Thomson Press (I) Ltd
C35 Phase-II.Noida

Contents

Foreword
by Ian Rankin

S tephen Fry once said of satirist Peter Cook that he was 'the funniest man who ever drew breath'. There's little doubt in my mind that Ron Ferguson is currently the funniest man drawing breath in Scotland.

He may even be the funniest man ever to have emerged (unscathed) from Cowdenbeath.

Like Ron, I was schooled in that fine town, and my first engagement with his writings came with the purchase of his book *Black Diamonds and the Blue Brazil*. Being a Fifer, I naturally sought out a second-hand copy, rather than paying the full admission rate, and then was surprised to see a family member, Alex Westwater, mentioned on the very first page. Scotland may contain multitudes, but it's a wee enough place for all that.

I've probably done Ron a mild disservice in comparing him to Peter Cook. Cook, after all, was a pure satirist, who always twisted the knife that little bit further. Ron, on the other hand, isn't just funny. He writes beautifully and compassionately about hot topics, and though, in arguments with his wife, he may 'pin his colours to the fence', in other debates he is fearless.

This sense of honesty and engagement would have served him well during his time in Fife, and afterwards as a kirk minister in Easterhouse. He brings a wealth of knowledge and insight to topics such as tsunamis and asylum seekers, abortion and sharia law, always treating a subject sensitively, intelligently, humanely, but with real candour, too. He also writes humorously (and often) about his passion for Cowdenbeath FC. Until now, I had thought myself alone in having attended Cowden reserve games as a lad. Something tells me Ron may have been a fellow sufferer.

For a year, back in the distant mists of time, I wrote a weekly column for a Sunday paper. I know how hard it can be to come up with the goods time and again. It seems to me that Ron's goal-scoring rate is exceptional. Here he is on all those reports penned by the likes of Lords Hutton and Butler: 'Britain may be less class-ridden than it once was, but tides of apparent reasonableness can still swamp sharp questions about public accountability'. This doesn't just strike me as apt, but is also elegantly proposed, the withering criticism hidden just below the surface (tucked away, in fact, in that crucial use of 'apparent'). Ron takes time over his craft, and as a result mines many diamonds of his own. But his words have the power to move, too, and when he talks of 'the awesome reality of sentient humanity' he is making a plea to each reader's sense of the spiritual.

Living in Orkney, Ron feels closer to the world of the spirit than most of us. I visit the place most years and know just what he means. It would be a foolish newspaper that didn't feel blessed by Ron's continuing contributions. The canny folk at the *Herald* are no fools. And now, thanks to the current collection of columns, even those who do not hark to the *Herald* can share the experience.

Ian Rankin
Edinburgh, 2005

Introduction

" **A** nd still they come, these collections of Herald columns, *Donald Dewar ate my Hamster, Hitler was a Vegetarian, Fear and Loathing in Lochgelly,* and now *Blue-Rinse Dreams and Banoffee Pie;* yes, they come in their thousands, millions even, from all over the world, part of a universal pilgrimage of grief...."

This take-off of a particularly naff, ubiquitous journalistic style is a coy way of saying that once more, in response to international, nay global, demand, Famedram has given birth to another compilation of recent columns, and I am right glad.

Writing newspaper columns is an odd business. The pressure of sitting in front of a blank screen on pre-publication day sets the adrenalin flowing. Words which are tapped out against the running of the clock on a Wednesday afternoon tend to make the writer wince at their printed frailty at breakfast time on Thursday.

"Writing is quite simple," observed Red Smith, the legendary American columnist and Pulitzer Prize winner. "All you have to do is sit down at your typewriter and open a vein."

Columns are all about opinions, often instant opinions; and about judgments, often sweeping judgments. Consistency, mercifully, is neither required nor, indeed, expected. What the columnist tries to do is to get "inside" public events and discern a trend, a cultural shift, an emergent paradigm, an inner meaning:

and then express these things in what is essentially a form of print entertainment, a piece of journalistic vaudeville. Today it's in print, tomorrow it's in the fire; unless, that is, it achieves a vulgar form of immortality by being included in an anthology.

Writing columns is a bit like initiating a conversation in a pub. Some people, simply enjoying a quiet drink, prick up their lugs when something controversial is said and find themselves moving over to listen to, and then join in, the discussion. Sometimes they agree with what the protagonist is saying; often they passionately disagree, and make their point forcibly. The letters and emails I receive express agreement, encouragement, disagreement and sometimes hostility. I reply to them all, and I learn a great deal in the process. I don't see my task as that of persuading people to agree with me; the columnist's proper job is surely to provoke readers to ask themselves questions about their own position on the matter under discussion.

Peter Jenkins, that outstanding political commentator, said that columnists spend a great deal of their time reading the papers on behalf of their readers, trying to make a pattern out of a torrent of words. He added that the job of the columnist was to take an ego trip to entertain the readers, "preferably by annoying them, with strong opinions on each and every subject."

Being a newspaper columnist is a privileged position. I get to inflict my prejudices on a grateful nation. And I get paid for it. No man but a blockhead, said Dr Johnson, ever wrote, except for money.

I would like to thank Ian Rankin for his most generous foreword. Scotland's biggest-selling novelist is not only a superb literary craftsman, he is a good and gracious human being. Even more, he is one of the Cowdenbeath Renaissance Men, along with the likes of

Nobel Prize Winner Sir James Black, Donald Findlay QC, Dennis Canavan MSP and Slim Jim Baxter.

Thanks also to the Glasgow Herald for permission to reproduce these pieces; and, in particular, to editor Mark Douglas-Home for his encouragement and executive editor Colin McDiarmid for the robustly stimulating Wednesday morning conversations about possible subjects for the next day's column.

My thanks once more to Bill McArthur for his classy illustrations for this series of books. At the 2005 Scottish Press Awards, his peers once more crowned him Cartoonist of the Year – the best in the business. And yet more thanks to Bill Williams, the hands-on proprietor of Famedram, for his enthusiastic and highly professional production of another volume.

".....And still they come......" etcetera, etcetera. I hope you enjoy reading these latest columns as much as I enjoyed doing the writing (and getting paid).

Ron Ferguson
Orkney 2005

The handy touch of genius

What do the following people have in common: Julius Caesar, Leonardo da Vinci, The Emperor Charlemagne, Alexander the Great, Ron Ferguson, Michelangelo, Joan of Arc, Napoleon Bonaparte, the Empress Josephine, Pablo Picasso? No, not everyone played for Cowdenbeath – only one achieved that eminence, and it wasn't Michelangelo on loan from AC Milan. The common factor is left-handedness.

But why, oh why, I hear you cry, did the Lord create left-handed people at all? I do have to point out, with a modest little Presbyterian cough, that the majority of lefthanders are touched with genius, but you will still be puzzled as to how it all fits in to the overall scheme of things.

For years, biologists have been mystified as to why such a significant minority of people – 10 per cent in Britain – should be born left-handed. This week, two researchers from the University of Montpellier came up with the conclusion that the more violence there was in a pre-industrial society, the greater the advantage of being left-handed. Charlotte Faurie and Michel Raymond compared homicide rates in eight native societies around the world, and they found that as the measure of violent aggression increased in each society, so did the proportion of men who are left-handed.

The surprise of left-handedness can give people an advantage in a fight. I always find that to be the case when I'm involved in a street brawl in Kirkwall. Even hulking opponents who are used to thrashing fellow right-handers tremble and cry for mercy when faced by the electronic crofter. They don't know where the next lethal blow is coming from – and that's only in the New Year Ba' game.

Did you know that in fortified houses, the stair is designed in such a way as to give the downrushing right-handed host an advantage? The laird hears an intruder downstairs and rushes down the spiral staircase with his trusty rapier in his right hand. The intruder is very constricted in his movements. When a pissed colonel meets a left-handed burglar, it's a much more equal, sporting, contest. Think about it.

But if left-handedness is nature's way of starting a fight, how come so many southpaws are geniuses? It's because we've had to find creative ways of living in a right-handed world. Many left-handers end up writing upside down to avoid blotting their copybook.

Can openers are a nightmare. I once failed to open a tin of dog meat in front of my starving, bewildered hound. I eventually took a hammer and chisel to the can, and ended up with meat and gravy running down the kitchen walls while the dug went mental. The electronic crofterina was not completely amused when she returned. It's hard being a misunderstood lefty.

Another reason for the prevalence of genius among left-handers is that we are discriminated against. It's not so long ago that children who wrote with their left hand were punished. Some even had their left hand tied behind their back. At primary school in Cowdenbeath I

2

was whipped, thrown into barrels of burning oil, compelled to crawl through steaming dung and thrown off high bridges into shark-infested waters, but I still persisted in writing with my left hand.

Left-handedness is largely hereditary. My mother was left-handed, and my brother is as well. Like myself, he is a genius, and modest with it. Older mothers are more likely to produce left-handed babies. My mother was well into her 30s when I emerged, a blinking prodigy, into the Fife coal dust.

I am a curiosity in that while I write and play tennis with my left hand (though not at the same time), and kick with my left foot (as they wouldn't say in the west of Scotland), I play golf right-handedly and play the guitar in the right-handed manner. I play the mouth organ by ear. Life can be confusing when you're a Renaissance Man.

Us persecuted southpaws also have to endure name-calling. We've always been derided. In Fife, it was "corrypaw'd" or "corrywheechit". The word "left" has always carried connotations of strangeness. It is derived from the Anglo-Saxon word, "lyft", which means "worthless". The Latin word for left is "sinister", which adds a weird dimension to us lefties. The Latin for "right", "dexter", implies skill and ease. The French for left is "gauche", which is not a compliment. It describes someone who is awkward and stumbling. Now while I occasionally break into silly walks, I don't collide with the furniture, even when I'm mentally working out equations which stumped Einstein.

What have the following got in common: President Harry S. Truman, Nelson Rockefeller, Rock Hudson, Her Majesty the Queen, Prince Charles, Marilyn Monroe, Fred Astaire, Steve McQueen, Johan Cruyff, Diego Maradona, Robert Redford, Paul Simon? You've got it in one.

3

The reason left-handers feel superior to right-handers is because we are. Sorry folks, but that's the way it is. And you disagree with us at your peril. Just remember that Jack the Ripper and the Boston Strangler were left-handers. Are you lookin' at me, Jimmy?

A town under seige

Today, two sets of young – and not so young – men will assemble at different parts of the city, prepared to march on the centre. All the shop windows will be boarded up in this old town under siege. Huge planks of wood will defy human entrance to side alleys.

The world's television cameras will roll as embedded reporters tell how the men are striding purposefully towards the conflict. Dressed in old clothes and toe-capped boots, the footsoldiers will be determined and focussed. They are men with a mission, prepared to give their all in the cause.

The city and royal burgh of Kirkwall is ready, as Saddam Hussein used to say before he got himself into a hole, for the mother of all battles. Welcome to Orkney's New Year's Day Ba' game.

When the gladiators reach the core of the Viking town, a big crowd of spectators – including visitors from many parts of the known world – will be assembled on the kirk green, in front of the imposing red-and-yellow sandstone St Magnus Cathedral. In the street, the two armies will face each other, ready to spring. All eyes will be on the Cathedral clock.

As the hands move near to 1pm, there will be shouts from the crowd. Then, as the clock strikes, a great roar will go up. A blurred brown and black leather ball will be hurled from the plinth in front of the Market cross. With flailing arms, the waiting men will throw themselves into action, scrabbling for the ball, which will immediately disappear into the heaving scrum.

Not a lot usually happens for a while. The spectators don't know where the ball is. Neither do most of the players. There is much shoving and sweating, with tactics being shouted in a curious code, often from the sidelines.

It's a very sociable occasion. Much fire-water is consumed. There will be people in the scrum who shouldn't be there because of age or medical history. They have promised their spouses that they will not take part, but somehow they find themselves in the game.

One person sure to be sucked into the steaming vortex will be Leslie Manson, Orkney's director of education. So will Bobby Leslie, chief librarian. They are good friends of mine, and they are completely off their heads on Ba' day.

Some old scores will be settled. People have been known to have bruises and broken ribs – and that's just the spectators. In previous years, the ball has ended up on roofs, pursued by the slavering pack. On one famous occasion, the game raged right through the middle of a local hotel. It stops for nothing or no one.

How did it all begin? No one is sure, since the written evidence is meagre. John Robertson, the foremost authority on the Ba', reveals in his magisterial book, "Uppies and Doonies", that football was played in Kirkwall's narrow streets in the early 17th century. The Ba' game cannot be traced earlier than the late 18th century.

There are some who seek to place it much earlier. The romantics would have its origins in a ritual

6

enactment of the ancient Sea Mither myth, in which the Mither, the great vital and creative force, eventually vanquishes the wintry-faced monster, Teran. The Norse sagas make mention of ball games, in which the heroes exhibit their daring and manliness.

Popular Kirkwall folklore locates the Ba' game in the ancient *Orkneyinga Saga*, in which the Orcadian Earl Sigurd defeats his rival, Maelbrigte Tusk, and takes his head back to Kirkwall. A poisoned tooth from the saddled head stabs Sigurd, who eventually dies.

As in *Sir Gawain and the Grene Knight,* a severed head makes a fine football. It's especially useful for dead ball situations.

In Orkney, everything begins in history and ends in mystery. My analytic head is with John Robertson, and my romantic heart is with the Sagas.

The game is contested between the town's Uppies and Doonies. The Uppies ('Up-the-Gates', derived from the Norse *gata*, meaning street) have to force the ball down to a particular street corner, while the Doonies have to get it into Kirkwall harbour. You are allowed to kick or lift the ball and run with it: apart from that there are few rules. It's a ferocious game, in which no quarter is asked or given.

Long after darkness has fallen, someone will pick up the severed Viking head and make a break. Irresistible ancient history will beckon him as he races through the winding Kirkwall streets until he reaches the gable end, or jumps into the freezing sea. Then the celebrations will begin in earnest. Old Firm, eat your heart out.

Through such corporate rituals, mythic history is re-enacted. In a not-so-holy communion, local community is remade, as hip flasks are passed reverently around. The Sea Mither will have vanquished the wintry Teran yet again, as the old earth shifts on her axis and an ancient promise is confirmed once more: the northern winter darkness will eventually make way for the glorious, never-ending, translucent light of an Orkney summer.

Osama and the flying Scottish Dronut

A doughnut is a doughnut is a doughnut. Wrong. The resemblances between a Scottish doughnut and an American doughnut are so slight as to cause one to ask whether there is any family connection whatsoever.

Your typical Scottish doughnut is in a class of its own. Mercifully. It is a big, round piece of concrete, dusted with flour. It may be several days, or even weeks, old, and it will certainly present a challenge both to your dentures and to your digestive system. The Scottish doughnut keeps the Scottish dentist in business.

A traditional, industrial-strength, Scottish doughnut is a weapon of mass destruction. The earliest evidence for this is to be found in the ancient scriptures. I have always been puzzled by the statement that David slew Goliath – who was about ten times the size of Bobo Balde – with a pebble. My diligent researches have established that this a mistranslation based on corrupted Hebrew consonants. The weapon was actually a month-old hairy Scottish doughnut. Fancy a doughnut, big man?

In Iraq, the Tony Blair political survival squadron should be looking for an innocent-looking small Scottish bakery on the outskirts of Basra. Stored there are piles of lethal Scottish floury ordnance.

9

The small Scottish doughnut may look harmless as it sails towards you, but it can cause concussion and disorientation. It is mainly used for crowd control. The medium doughnut – the 'Caledoughnut' – fired from a rocket holder, can cause severe injury and even death. The Cruise doughnut will destroy vast territories when dropped from a B 45.

The unmanned flying Scottish "dronut" is a magnificent search-and-destroy weapon. This is the missile which should have been used in the Boro Boro caves of Afghanistan. Osama bin Laden would not have survived an attack by a Scottish doughnut flying at near ground level.

An American doughnut is totally different. It is light, and melts in the mouth. At the time of purchase, your doughnut will have been made within the past hour. (Within the hour! I dare you to go into a Scottish baker's, point to a whiskery doughnut, and ask, in a fake American accent, if it was produced within the last hour. The shop will be destroyed by gales of laughter.)

Here in America, you can watch your own personal doughnut being made, then glazed, before being popped, still warm, into your own salivating mouth. Your personal doughnut! I know, because I've just been doing it. Along with excited, baseball cap-wearing children, I watched my own doughnut move from conception through full term in less two minutes, before I fell upon it in a devouring frenzy.

Doughnuts which are not consumed in a short time are given away to the poor and hungry. Which is why you will find your electronic crofter, dressed as a tramp, accompanied by an Alsatian, outside a Krispy Kreme shop in North Carolina. I beat the dog to the doughnuts every time.

I tell you, these doughnuts are addictive. The American Revolution was worth it, just for this. It's right there in the Declaration of Independence. Every human being has the right to a decent doughnut.

The reason I'm telling you all this is because it has just been announced that the fastest-growing dining category in America is the doughnut shop. It had a 9.6 per cent sales growth last year.

The three fastest-growing doughnut chains, Dunkin' Donuts, Krispy Kreme and Tim Horton's, all reported big profit jumps. Experts attribute the growth to consumers' desire for small indulgences during stressful times. Al Qaeda would seem to be the marketing arm of the American doughnut business.

Nutritionists are alarmed. Doughnuts are deep-fried, glazed, and crammed with calories. "There's no redeeming quality in a doughnut," pontificated Hope Warshaw, editor of *A Guide to Healthy Restaurant Eating*, and a right wee puritan.

I like the comment of Scott Livengood – no, the name is not made up – chief executive of Krispy Kremes.

"We've never called ourselves a health food, and don't pretend to be."

The downside of the American doughnut is that what melts in the mouth goes straight to the waist. There is a serious obesity problem here in the land of the fry, and the evidence is before your eyes. Some Americans resemble nothing more than gigantic doughnuts wearing shorts. You see whole families of doughnuts going about their lawful business.

Mind you, we in Britain are in no place to cast the first doughnut. We have our own high proportion of European food mountains on legs. Obesity is rampant in Albion, and it is a serious health hazard. The Labour party, which is essentially the puritan wing of the political system, is threatening sanctions against wilful guzzlers. Where is Bessie Braddock now that we need her?

It's just as well that I'm only here in North Carolina for six weeks. The electronic crofter's well-deserved reputation for having a svelt and lithe frame – the body of a god, really – would soon take a bit of a battering.

Here is the shameful truth: the crofter's legendary moral fibre is being inexorably undermined by a small circle of utterly decadent, utterly irresistible, deep-fried, glazed calories. Moral death by Krispy Kreme. A gloriously unPresbyterian way to go.

Beware of Geeks Bearing Spiffs

B eggars can be choosers, it seems. The scruffy, half-shaven man at the street corner holding out his bowl towards you may not be a homeless vagrant, but a top businessman on retreat. He may even be the manager from the bank which likes to say Yes but has said a pin-striped No to your request for a loan, or a wan computer whiz-kid who has dressed down into stinking rags while smoking wacky baccy. Beware of geeks bearing spiffs.

What's all this about? Well, a new concept called the "street retreat" is about to hit Britain. It's been going for a few years in the United States, and applications are being taken now for the first event to be held in London next month. Scotland will be next in line.

Offered by church groups and organisations such as the Hudson River Peacemaker Centre in New York, the street retreat gives stressed-out executives an opportunity to experience life on the city streets. It is intended to be a spiritual journey with a difference. Rather than offering people a weekend of pampering at a spa, the organizers expose retreatants to some less than salubrious experiences.

What happens is this. Participants pay a modest fee to take part in the three to five day event. They are asked to refrain from shaving and washing their hair for five days before the retreat. Old clothes (only one set) are to be worn. Money, watches, books and mobile phones are not permitted. You can bring only an empty bag for collecting food from shelters.

The Peacemaker Centre has been organising the retreats on the streets of New York for the past few years. "You have one piece of ID, no money and you are living on the streets," Francisco Lugovina, a Zen Buddhist teacher at the centre, says. "You do not know where you are going to get your next meal. You rely on asking people on the streets where the free lunches and the shelter can be found and you find they are very generous."

Genro Gauntt, an experienced leader, will be in charge of the London event on the weekend of 24 to 26 June. The fee will be £150, and no more than 18 people will be allowed to join in. The group will split up during the day to beg for money and look for food. Everyone will reunite at night to sleep together.

Charley Cropley, 57, a doctor in Boulder, Colorado, was on a street retreat in downtown Denver in March.

"It's hard for me to tell you how grateful I felt to people who gave me money," he said. "You think people despise you, yet so many people are not that way. The people that give you food at the shelters – what would you do without them? You would die without people's kindness. And there's nothing in it for them. There's no explanation for it. It's just kindness."

Glasgow next? Are Alsatians provided? This piece of theatre will soon be showing at street corner near you. The big issue, so to speak, is this: Is this just self-indulgent nonsense indulged in by precious people, with nothing better to do with their time, or is it a serious

14

attempt to expose spiritually starving pilgrims to potentially life-changing experiences?

Before we come to a judgment, let me take you back a few years to the Iona Community's old headquarters in Clyde Street, Glasgow. Community House's rooms resounded to talk of social justice. People like Jimmy Reid, Bruce Millan, George Thomson and Dickson Mabon cut their political teeth there. Some of the sharpest minds of their generation, like R.D. Laing, Walter Fyfe and Geoff Shaw were frequent visitors. When Rev Douglas Alexander was warden, his two children, Wendy and Douglas, inhaled radical Christian thinking.

Under the wardenship of the Rev Campbell Robertson, Community House's café was frequented by Glasgow's down-and-outs. Robertson's ministry among the poor was exceptional. He instituted a foot-washing service for stinking dossers. His work with Glasgow's homeless – supported by the visionary Fred Edwards, head of Strathclyde Region's social work department – was legendary, and his early death was a great loss.

As part of their joining induction, new members of the Iona Community were let loose on the streets of Glasgow with little money in their pockets, and told to survive. For some it was transformational. Out of all these strands of practical thinking, the Community developed Columban Houses - little communities of volunteers who would live in hard-to-let houses in tough areas.

If the proposed street retreats are merely radical-chic designer-hobo gimmicks, then they are an abomination. Street people should not be audio-visual aids for anyone's ego trip towards a fresh supply of dining-out stories. Disembodied, untroublesome, pseudo-spirituality, divorced from practical compassion, is an indulgence.

15

If, on the other hand, the desire is for an opening of eyes and heart, as part of a spiritual transformation which will refresh the wellsprings of social conscience in an era of consumer-sickness, then let me take you through the streets of Glasgow, where you'll be shown something to remake your mind.

Presbyterian parrot that refused to swear

A friend of mine in Glasgow has an ageing, squawking parrot. Every time I phone Graham, Billy can be heard fulminating in the background. This is no shy and retiring bird. Billy is a loud conversationalist who enjoys the sound of his own voice.

Billy actually belonged to Graham's uncle. The old man was driven to distraction by his loquacious companion. When the World Cup was on television, Billy squawked through the commentary. The football lover, having failed to shut the wretched bird up by putting a cover over the cage, got up in a fury and threw bird and cage out of the door. A few minutes later, there was a knock at the door. "Haw sur," said an urchin with one eye on a reward, "dae ye ken yer burd's flew oot wi' its cage on?".

Chastened owner 0, Parrot 1, after extra time.

The bird had to go. Graham was the lucky winner.

I used to visit an elderly lady who had a remarkable parrot. He was a wonderful mimic. His owner told me that some mischievous workmen tried to teach the parrot some sweary words. They wanted to shock and embarrass the respectable churchgoing matron. Ah, but virtue won. "He absolutely refused to swear," said my hostess, triumphantly.

17

I like that word "refused". This was a Presbyterian parrot, not to be swayed from the paths of righteousness. It's good to know that there is at least one creature, great or small, holding the line. As far as I am aware, it is still declining to use bad language.

Not so, it would appear, with Sir Winston Churchill's parrot. This week's sensational news, by courtesy of the *Mirror* – so it must be true – is that the war leader's female parrot, Charlie, would roundly curse the enemy. Her favourite sayings were "F*** Hitler" and "F*** the Nazis". Even today, 39 years after the great man's death, she can still be coaxed into repeating them.

Charlie, who is now 104 years old, was bought by Peter Oram for his pet shop after Churchill died in 1965. He was forced to move her into his home after she kept swearing at children. For the last 12 years, she has lived at Mr Oram's garden centre in Reigate, Surrey.

Centre worker Sylvia Martin said: "If truth be told, Charlie is looking a little scruffy but she is very popular with the public. We are all very attached to her." James Humes, an expert on the late prime minister, commented: "Churchill may no longer be with us but that spirit and those words of defiance and resolve continue."

The blue and gold macaw is believed to be Britain's oldest bird. It is reported that visiting dignitaries were shocked by the tirades from the cage, though the prime minister did not conceal his enjoyment at their discomfiture. Oh to be a fly on the wall when the Archbishop of Canterbury came to visit! All creatures great and small, the Lord God made them all. Now we know who it was who helped the inspiring war leader get through Britain's darkest hour.

A mimicking bird can be a complete menace. I heard only yesterday of a couple whose Minah bird did a superb imitation of a telephone ringing. The feathered pest with a devilish sense of humour drove them crazy. It didn't quite fly oot wi' its cage on, but it departed the scene by more orthodox means.

Listening in to the parrots of famous people would obviously be very revealing, so this column instructed its team of researchers to eavesdrop on the birds of the great and the good. Let's begin with my great and good self. In the middle of profound and deeply meaningful discussions in the electronic croft, my parrot interjects, for some unaccountable reason, "C'mon the Blue Brazil!". The bird is the subject of mysterious assaults which put the Stephen Hawking puzzles into the shade. An unseen intruder apparently tries to throttle my beloved pet. As I search high and low for the culprit, the electronic crofterina has a strange look in her eyes.

Jack McConnell's parrot was inherited from the late Donald Dewar, and says "um" and "er" all the time. It has recently started declaring, "To be perfectly frank". Geoff Hoon's bird keeps pacing up and down in its cage, muttering, "How can I survive this?" – to which the obvious answer is, "With body armour". Pity there's none left.

Ally McCoist's sick parrot agonises, "I must stop playing away from home". The Queen's bird, called Annis Horribilis, says nothing indiscreet, but Prince Philip's parrot does less than hilarious take-offs of stupid Indian waiters.

I can report exclusively that George W. Bush's parrot actually lives in London, England. The president gives it a pat on the head when making state visits to London, or when his favourite pet is brought to see him in Washington. Tony is a slightly vain bird with a bright plumage. Desperately keen to please, he repeats his master's bad language at every opportunity. Oh how I wish he had the moral fibre to refuse.

19

Partnership made in heaven

T
he stranger is brought by car to Rackwick Bay, perhaps Orkney's most stunning piece of visual theatre. The sheer cliffs of Hoy stand in their rugged majesty, as the waves crash against the gorgeous sandy beach. Ruined cottages speak nostalgically of crofting and fishing. There is drizzle in the air on this summer's day, in the year of Our Lord, 1970. There is about to be a momentous meeting, one which will influence Orkney's future – though no one, least of all the participants, understands this at the time.

The handsome visitor, in his early 30s, had discovered, as he stepped ashore, that George Mackay Brown was also to be on Hoy that afternoon. The visitor was intrigued: the day before he had come upon the Orcadian poet's book, *An Orkney Tapestry,* in a local bookshop, and had been so enchanted that he had stayed up all night in the Kirkwall Hotel until he reached the final page.

Thanks to a chance encounter at the Lyness pierhead, the stranger was invited to lunch at Mucklehoose, a cottage near the shore at Rackwick. Now he enters the cottage, then introduces himself to another lunch guest, a shy man with a chiselled face. Peter Maxwell Davies meets George Mackay Brown.

Thus began the partnership of two men who were destined to become giants in their chosen fields. So entranced was he by the wild Orkney seascapes that Maxwell Davies accepted an invitation to return to Mucklehoose to write the score for Ken Russell's film, *The Devils*. He was hooked. He was home.

Mackay Brown pointed out an abandoned house at the top of the cliff at Rackwick, with 60 years of sheep muck inside. Once restored, this was to be the composer's island eyrie for more than 25 years. It was in this house, exposed to the tumultuous Hoy storms, that Maxwell Davies would compose the symphonies which made his name as one of the greatest composers of his generation. Meanwhile, in a Council house in Stromness, Mackay Brown was scribbling, in a ruled notebook, the poems, short stories and novels which would bring him international recognition and many awards.

With co-founders Norman Mitchell, organist and music master at St Magnus Cathedral, and Stromness schoolteacher Archie Bevan, Max inspired the St Magnus Festival. It began in 1977 with the production of PMD's work, *The Martyrdom of St Magnus*, scripted by George Mackay Brown. Many festivals were to feature Maxwell Davies-Mackay Brown collaborations.

When the music of Peter Maxwell Davies was first played to Orcadian audiences, the punters looked around at each other in bewilderment. The avant-guard, dissonant, music was not easy to grasp first time around. Nor second time around. It certainly wasn't stuff you would whistle on the way home.

The story in Orkney is that during one concert, someone shouted from the balcony, "When will the orchestra stop tuning up?". Maxwell Davies, who was wielding the baton, rushed upstairs, rebuked the patron,

21

then scooted back down and started at the beginning again.

What eventually won Orcadians over was the gloriously accessible music he also wrote. He composed wonderful music for local children, set to the words of his soulmate, GMB. And audiences became educated to the point of appreciating his more challenging works.

As the fame of Peter Maxwell Davies and George Mackay Brown burgeoned, so did the St Magnus Festival. From a fragile, low-key, weekend event, it flourished into a six-day extravangaza. PMD just picked up the phone, and the big orchestras and soloists headed for Orkney. You could run into Isaac Stern, Vladimir Askenazy, Ronnie Scott, Evelyn Glennie, and Tommy Smith in Kirkwall's Broad Street.

GMB likewise worked his magic. Naomi Mitchison, Norman McCaig, Ronald Mavor, Ted Hughes, Stewart Conn, Edwin Morgan, Iain Crichton Smith and Seamus Heaney held the Orcadian wordsmith in such esteem that they didn't need a second asking.

Local musicians, actors and dancers jostled with the big names on the programme, because St Magnus Festival is still, at its heart, a community festival. That is how PMD and GMB wanted it. That is also why last night's 70th birthday concert in honour of the composer was such an exuberant love-in.

How we need inspired Makars to help our lives make deeper connections!

One memory in particular stays with me. George Mackay Brown contrived to die in time to be buried on St Magnus Day, 16th April, 1996. At the service in St Magnus Cathedral, I was able to welcome a huge congregation which resembled cast from a GMB short story. After the requiem mass, Peter Maxwell Davies sat down quietly at the Steinway and played his exquisite

Farewell to Stromness. There was not a dry eye in the house of God.

As I sit in the electronic croft, while that same music plays, I look across the short stretch of water to Hoy, and meditate upon that quixotic, unplanned, meeting at Rackwick 34 years ago. Chance encounter? To quote that turbulent Celtic theological Makar, George MacLeod, "If you call that a coincidence, I wish you a very dull life."

Graveyard voice which says "J'accuse"

I magine this scene. You're out with family and close friends at a celebration in a local pub. The company is convivial and the drink is flowing. At closing time, nobody wants to go home, so you invite them back to the house. Wine and beer and the best single malts are brought out. The stories and the banter continue till the early hours, at which point one of the guests indicates that he's going to drive home.

You know that he's had a bucketful, and shouldn't be driving. You invite him to stay overnight, but he says he needs to get back home. You plead with him, but he insists that he is fit to drive. He closes the door, and you hear the car engine rev up. What do you do next?

For many readers, this scenario – or one with more than a passing resemblance to it – will not be entirely unfamiliar. Many of us will have been in situations where a family member or friend has got behind the wheel in less than safe circumstances. Maybe we've done it ourselves, and have got home safely. Or not.

A court case in France this week has divided the country. The story is this. Jean-Sébastien Fraisse, aged 31, and his wife, 29-year-old Angélique, invited friends back to their house after a celebration at a local cafe. More drink was consumed at the house. Then at four in the morning, their friend Frédéric Colin, aged 29, announced that he was going to drive home. Knowing how much alcohol he had consumed, the couple tried without success to persuade him to stay overnight. After leaving their flat in Moselle, in eastern France, Colin drove three miles down the wrong side of a main road before hitting another car head-on, killing himself and a couple and two of their three children.

The grandmother of the only surviving child, aged five, launched a private prosecution, claiming that the couple should have done more to stop their guest from driving, and could at least have called the police when he insisted. But the public prosecutor recommended acquittal, arguing it would not be desirable to set a legal precedent requiring people to inform on their friends.

The verdict of the court was that the couple were not guilty of charges of failing to prevent a crime involving bodily harm. A profound irony of the case is that Angélique Fraisse was herself run over by a drink-driver when she was 16 and is now paraplegic.

Well, what do you think? What would you have done in the circumstances? It's worth recalling the biblical story of Cain, who kills and buries his brother, Abel. Cain protests that he doesn't know where Abel is, and asks: "Am I my brother's keeper?". The Lord responds: "What hast thou done? The voice of thy brother's blood crieth unto me from the ground."

This issue is far from simple. Suppose your son failed to heed your warnings about drink and drove off in his (or even your) car. Should you/would you "shop" him to the police, with the consequence that he would lose his driving licence? In some respects it might be easier to stop a member of your family than to do so in the case of a friend, but consider the situation of a wife whose violent husband regularly drives over the limit. If she lets the authorities know, she will be bruised, if not dead, meat.

There are other angles to this. Do bar staff who serve drink to an already over-the-limit driver, knowing that he has a car outside, bear any responsibility if he ploughs into a bus queue on the way home? Are they their punter's keeper? Discuss.

We tend to think that individual adults must stand or fall by their own choices. But the problem with drink-driving is that too much alcohol impairs the judgment of the individual to the extent that he or she is indignantly convinced that it is perfectly safe to drive. In which case other adults have a responsibility to intervene. Put it this way: if you were the grandparent in the case in question, would you not feel that those who watched the perpetrator drive off were culpable, and should face consequences under the law? I do.

I believe that Jean-Sébastien or Angélique Fraisse should have lifted the telephone and called the police the minute their friend left the house. Part of the reason I feel so strongly about this is that in my time I have buried too many young people. I also believe that the law should reflect that culpability. The sentence can take into account all mitigating circumstances.

There are times when humanity – if not God – demands that we have to take adult responsibility and be our brother's keeper, as he might have to be ours at other times. If we duck it, even if the law fails to do its job, the voice which rises from the flower-strewn ground will rightly say "J'accuse".

Knit your own nutter

Y ou don't have to be a weirdo to be a Christian, but it helps. That's the impression you might get from the depiction of religious believers on television. The stereotype is of a slightly deranged, starey-eyed, censorious fanatic who looks down from the moral high ground on sinners who are, praise the Lord, headed for eternal damnation.

TV soap operas are, in many respects, modern morality plays in which the baddies, after many twists and turns in the increasingly preposterous ratings-driven plots, usually get their comeuppance. Unlike the medieval passion stories, however, the Christians are normally the least appealing characters around. A particular example is Dot Cotton in EastEnders. Picky, old fashioned, spewing Bible texts and putting mere mortals in their place, she is the neighbour from hell who is certain she's going to heaven.

I'm not a great television fan, but I saw the first episode of the new BBC sitcom, My Family. The script was funny, but it featured the mandatory Christian bampot. The born-again son, with his witless chorus-singing pals, was a classic, knit-your-own religious nutter. You could make it up – from the colour-in handbook of holy heidbangers. It's so awful it gives caricaturing a bad name.

For some reason, even good TV scriptwriters can get away with lazy clichés when it comes to religion. Think about it. When did you last see a television drama in which a religious believer had his or her full complement of marbles, never mind doing something moderately good in the world?

There are two possible, if not entirely serious, candidates. Father Ted is an amusing, warm, character – almost sane, compared with every other dribbling or psychopathic priest who lives in his establishment. The Vicar of Dibley is a positive, funny, portrayal of a cleric who is not a goody two-shoes and enjoys her life in the parish and community. Mind you, most of the characters who pass through the vicarage are unhinged.

Dr Ailsa Hollinshead, the newly appointed chair of the Religious Advisers' Committee for Scottish and Grampian TV, has highlighted the clichés. She knows what she's talking about – she studied the portrayal of Christians on TV for her doctorate. Results from focus groups, made up of Christians, Sikhs, Muslims and non-religious people, reported that positive depictions of Christianity in drama are hard to find.

Hollinshead is also concerned about the lack of accurate characters from minority faiths. Her focus groups found an assumption that any storyline with a Muslim character in it would predictably involve an arranged marriage, an oppressive father, or racist incidents.

The stereotyping goes wider than television. Composer James MacMillan has justifiably complained about the way Roman Catholics are often portrayed. He should try being a Calvinist. In our benighted wee country, Calvinists are held personally responsible for male chauvinism, cultural Philistinism, the gloomy Scottish disposition, long working hours, national outbreaks of hemorrhoids, and the weather. We still have posturing Scottish writers who portray themselves as heroic battlers against the Calvinist establishment – even though Scottish Calvinists are now a protected species. How do these subsidized poseurs get away with this intellectual sloth?

Today, you would get carried off by the thought police if you caricatured blacks, midgets, gays, or Afghan asylum seekers – unless they were Christians. A lesbian Scottish international footballer with a wooden leg would only be pilloried if she were self-confessedly "born-again".

Now, I've met quite a few crazed Christians in my time. I've encountered a number of religious video nasties. Some of them write to me, assuring me – with the love of Jesus burning in their hearts, of course – that I'm bound for eternal fiery furnaces. I have to say, though, that I've met numberless ordinary, decent religious believers who've made a pretty good fist of loving their neighbour, and even their enemies. Many have inspired me by their utterly wonderful self-giving loving. I could write a very large book about non-celebrities I've known who have exhibited awesome qualities.

To be labeled as a Christian in some quarters is to be regarded automatically as brain dead, or as having been at the head of the queue when the free frontal lobotomies were being performed. Yet I've known religious believers of great intellectual power: our own Professor Iain Torrance – who is about to become president of the prestigious Princeton Seminary – and Archbishop Rowan Williams spring immediately to mind.

I've been inspired by radical Scottish Christians like Geoff Shaw, George MacLeod, Sister Isobel Smythe, John Smith, Alice Scrimgeour, Bob Holman, John and Mary Miller, Margaret Forrester, and Father Willy Slavin.

29

All this without looking at the Martin Luther Kings and the Mother Teresas.

Having made the point, let me finally confess an ambivalence about this whole 'Christian' business. As I witness the recrudescence of bitter religious fundamentalism and the unlistening, disrespectful posture of an American empire which presents itself as the vanguard of Christian civilization, I feel that the word 'Christian' now carries too much baggage to be helpfully descriptive. It has become too disengaged from the man from Nazareth to be truthful. Caricature is one thing: but the deeper problem lies here.

Mercy for a mass murderer?

On a windswept hillside on the island of Hoy in Orkney there lies a little grave. It is the last resting place of a local girl, Betty Corrigall. She was betrothed to a sailor, who abandoned her after she became pregnant. Betty committed suicide rather than face the shame. People who took their own lives were felt by the Church to have committed an unpardonable sin, and they were not allowed burial in consecrated ground. Standing at that bleak graveside, you cannot help but experience waves of pity.

But what about Dr Harold Shipman, who took his own life in Wakefield prison on Tuesday? What kind of emotions does that evoke? The Sun newspaper is in no doubt. Its banner front page headline yesterday was unambiguous. "Ship, Ship Hooray!" it proclaimed.

Is the death of Harold Shipman a tragedy in the way that the suicide of Betty Corrigall was? Before we move to that judgment, it's necessary to look at some important aspects of the case. Shipman was suspected of being responsible for a total of 215 murders. While the relatives of the victims will not be awash with tears, many will be bitterly disappointed that any possible opportunity for hearing details of the cases which didn't come to court is now gone.

In effect, Harold Shipman committed capital punishment on himself. Predictably, there have been renewed calls for the restoration of the death penalty. But surely one of the things we learned in the 20th century is that miscarriages of justice are not entirely infrequent. Posthumous apology after wrongful execution by the state provides little solace.

Could Shipman's suicide have been averted? It is the prison service's duty to keep safe all prisoners committed to its care. However, there are limits to what the authorities can do. It is impossible to stop even those who are subject to suicide watch from doing the deed. Someone with Dr Shipman's medical knowledge and mastery of deception would be able to outwit his captors.

What is curious is the speed with which investigative action was taken. The inquiry actually began yesterday. In Scotland, we have had several suicides amongst young people in prison, some of whom were on remand. It is impossible to escape the conclusion that Shipman's notoriety made him something of a "celebrity" prisoner. In the media age, immediate public action was deemed essential.

Why did Shipman take his own life? The received view is that this ruthless, calculating, man was determined to be in control, right till the end. This may well be the correct explanation. Or it may simply be true that, facing the knowledge that he would never be released, Shipman decided that he could not face an unending life under lock and key.

There is an issue here which needs to be addressed. Only some 20 of the 74,000-plus currently in prison are serving natural life sentences. All the others will probably come out. Throw away the key and you throw away hope. Life imprisonment without end might appeal to populist politicians, but it virtually removes the possibility of redemption. It's time for a rethink.

So is Shipman's suicide a tragedy? Given the enormity of his crimes, it is hard to see it as such. The nation has not lost one of its treasures. He was not a big enough man to face his crimes, co-operate with the police, and apologize to the relatives of his victims, thus giving them at least a degree of closure.

There are dimensions to all this, though, which go way beyond the juridical. We are all accountable to God. The man who played God will have to face the one who does not play God. There will be no scope for dissembling.

People often shout, "Rot in hell, you bastard!" at a person convicted of serious crimes. It's become a tabloid cliché. What kind of judgment can Harold Shipman expect? Will he rot in hell? One of the things I learned in my days as a minister was that you never really know the true inner story of someone's life. As a biographer, too, the ultimate frustration is that no matter how many facts you have assembled, you do not have access to your subject's innermost thought processes. In fact, most of us have a hard enough time becoming familiar with our own inner make-up.

In the biblical tradition, Moses, the heroic leader of the exodus from Egypt was a murderer. The patriarch Jacob was a swindler and a crook. Israel's greatest king, David, was an adulterer who, when his mistress became pregnant, had her husband sent out to the front line to certain death. The Bible is a rogues' gallery. Its testimony is that the ultimate force of the universe is a God of love. Even his judgment is a form of tough love.

Will God throw away the final key for Harold Shipman? Will there be mercy even for a mass murderer? It's none of my business, but I hope so. If there is, there may be hope for thee and me: and poor Betty Corrigall as well.

33

Lambie and rice on the Middle East menu

John Lambie should be flown out to the Middle East to help Condoleezza Rice with the peace process.

The cigar-smoking, pigeon-loving, former Partick Thistle manager, who is a natural spokesman for Tourette's Syndrome Anonymous, could form a dream ticket with the entrancing, intriguing Condi. Why? We'll come to that in a minute.

First let's talk about a bizarre mental condition called Jerusalem Syndrome. It afflicts a considerable number of visitors to Jerusalem who, the minute they set foot on holy soil, become convinced they are characters from the Bible. Some start preaching in the streets or dancing like King David before the ark of the covenant. Others walk around naked, or head out to the river Jordan with a view to baptizing, or even crucifying, any punters who are hanging about.

Dr Moshe Kalian, the district psychiatrist of Jerusalem, who has diagnosed many cases of the psychosis, said: "There are anecdotal cases, like a tourist who was making a fuss in a hotel because he was giving orders to prepare the Last Supper. There was a lady who went to an emergency room, claimed she was having a miscarriage and when the doctors told her she was not pregnant at all, she said she came to Jerusalem to give birth to the new baby Jesus."

It should be noticed that strange behaviour has been going on for aeons. About two centuries after Christ, a group of zealots in Jerusalem were convinced that the world was coming to an end. They climbed to the top of Masada – the place where Jewish martyrs had once committed suicide rather than submit to the enemy – and awaited the End. Well, it came. They all died of sunstroke.

The attention is back on Jerusalem today. The divided holy city is at the heart of the Israeli-Palestinian struggle. It is an awe-full city of aspiration and madness. It is a jangling, dangerous theatre of the absurd and the sublime. Enter, pilgrim, at your peril. If the mini messiahs don't get you, the ultra-violet rays will.

Two men who shook hands yesterday now hold the peace of Jerusalem in their hands. These two leaders are imprisoned by memories – of wilderness wanderings, promised land, unspeakable Holocaust, postwar terrorism, ejection from homelands, suicide bombings, imprisonment without trial, provocative settlements and groaning injustice. Sharon and Abbas will either rewrite history, or end up as insignificant historical footnotes. They have to find a way of squaring a circle which must contain two viable neighbouring states, reinforced by credible guarantees about security; and they must resolve fraught questions about the governance of Jerusalem and the number of returning refugees.

Ariel Sharon and Mahmoud Abbas have no need to take on Jerusalem fantasies. They are already high profile actors in a biblical drama with very high stakes. The devil will be in the detail, but there's a lot more to it than that. If there is to be a binding solution, Sharon and Abbas could do with a touch of divine madness, a piece of non-Jerusalem Syndrome which lifts them out of their geographical and historical imprisonments and enables them to imagine that they are other people.

Which other people? Let's say FW de Klerk and Nelson Mandela. No, I'm not saying the Israel/Palestine situation is identical to the South African impasse. It isn't. But as well as a detailed righting of wrongs, the South African settlement required the willingness of two foes to stand outside of their traditions and imagine a new thing.

De Klerk read the runes, and had the courage to take off his own tribal blinkers. Mandela somehow found within himself the generous capacity to put years of imprisonment in Robben Island behind him and to reach out to his captors and enemies. Thus was a bloodbath averted, and a country empowered to embark on a long and still dangerous journey towards stability.

Can Ariel Sharon and Mahmoud Abbas imagine themselves into new and unpredicted ways of being? Can they allow themselves to make an imaginative leap of faith which will take them out of habitual roles and enable them to try on the mantles of a de Klerk or a Mandela, a Martin Luther King or a John F Kennedy? Such an inspired and historic compromise would need, of course, to be backed by American might and money. Shalom – justice with peace – in the Middle East would be cheap at the price.

Condoleezza Rice would make an unlikely wise and patient Solomon. But this is where Lambie the motivational magician comes in. In one of John's innumerable incarnations as Partick Thistle manager, a less-than-skilful player was carried off with concussion. When the trainer reported that the player didn't know who he was, Lambie snarled, "Tell him he's Pele and send him back on."

Will Sharon and Abbas raise their game in a championship which needs to end win-win? There is everything to play for in front of a watching world which should cheer them on, while insisting that the playing field is nothing less than level.

Opportunity Knox for purple knickers

The statue of John Knox may bear a frown on Saturday morning. In the setting of the Kirk's historic assembly hall, the temporary home of Scotland's new parliament, Scottish history will be made. As commissioners from all over Scotland stand to attention at the cry of 'Moderator', the chosen leader who walks down the aisle will be neither – shock! horror! – male nor ordained.

The purple knickers have been a long time in coming. The first female Moderator – and the first elder to sit in the historic chair of plain Mr Knox for more than 400 years – will be in the spotlight for the next 12 months, representing the Church of Scotland at home and abroad.

Richard Holloway, former Scottish Episcopal Primus, famously described opponents of women's ordination as 'miserable buggers'. Well, Dr Alison Elliot will have a few miserable buggers on her case for the next 12 months, hoping for slip-ups which will support their argument that church leadership is a man's business. I predict that they will be disappointed.

Now, so far as predictions are concerned, the electronic crofter is your man. With an endearingly modest cough, this column can point to two separate successful pre-season public forecasts of promotion for Cowdenbeath Football Club – decided, on both occasions, in the last game of the season – as well as to his correctly prophesied elevation of the outsider John Miller to the Moderatorial chair. And, following a scrutiny of Viking runes at the Standing Stones of Stenness, your man from the north pole predicted that the Rev Margaret Forrester would come closer than the pundits were suggesting last year. It went to a second ballot. And in *The Herald* of 23rd August, 2001, after examining the diseased entrails of an Orcadian badger, Kirkwall's Kierkegaard spake thus (about women Moderators) unto a grateful nation: "This column's dark horse outsider to make the Moderatorial breakthrough is Dr Alison Elliot, who is – Crivvens! Two taboos for the price of one! – not even a minister. Maybe not this year, but soon. What fun! Remember you read it first in *The Herald.*"

What Alison Elliot's appointment does is to make an unambiguous public statement that men and women are equal in the ministry of the Kirk. Not only will the high profile of the 55-year-old mother of two affirm women and elders, it will provide encouragement for women and lay people in other denominations.

The present pope has banned discussion of the ordination of women, never mind the role of women in leadership. That conversation will not go away, however, even if John Paul II is succeeded by Pope Canute I. Lurking at the back of all of this are some very dodgy clerical attitudes to women. The greatest of Catholic theologians, St Thomas Aquinas, opined: "As regards the individual nature, woman is defective and misbegotten." Well, that's youse telt. This echoes Samuel Johnson's view: "Sir, a woman preaching is like a dog's walking on his hinder legs. It is not done well: but you are surprised to find it done at all."

But things do change. Look again at Rangers Football Club. Nowadays, there are more people crossing themselves at Ibrox than at Lourdes.

What will Dr Elliot face on Saturday? One of the dictionary definitions of moderator is "a device for the regulation of the flow of gas." There will be plenty around in the Assembly hall this week. The temptation when you're up against it is to go out and do something, anything. One of the great siren voices is that of "modernisation". The temptation should be resisted.

Why? Modernisation, in its contemporary meaning, is an ideology. It's a false god. It promises improvement and delivers chaos. It concentrates on management, efficiency and image. Its great nostrum is reorganisation. It goes for targets, rebranding, and spindoctoring – the kind of guff which has bedevilled the health services. We haven't got to short-term ministerial contracts linked to bonuses for baptisms, weddings and funerals – yet.

When in doubt, reorganise. Here is a text for Assembly commissioners, as they prepare to debate yet more organisational reshuffling. It comes from Gaius Petronius in the year AD 66: "We tend to meet any new situation by reorganising. What a wonderful method it can be for creating the illusion of progress, while producing confusion, inefficiency and demoralisation."

Here's a better word than modernisation: reformation. It's about living out a core message in new and imaginative ways. Endless debates about reorganisation are a diversion from the primary task. The crisis of the Church is theological, not organisational.

The election of a woman Moderator is about good theology, about redeeming the historically distorted relationship between women and men in the community

40

of faith. Reformation involves a radical contemporary conversation with the mothers and fathers of the faith, on a 21st century Scottish spiritual journey which – unlike modernisation with its obsessive technological 'fixes' for every 'problem' – has no detailed route map. When such an unapologetic spiritual adventure is embarked upon with boldness, many strange and interesting fellow-travellers, dissatisfied with the ill-nourishing husks of postmodern nihilism, will join the pilgrimage.

Tribal dreamings at the birth of a boy

We are a grandfather. Daniel Joseph David Ferguson has made his debut appearance on earth, and my heart is right glad. Weighing in at 9lb 2oz, the boy already looks like a take-no-prisoners Cowdenbeath centre half. Called after my father, Joe Ferguson, this robust, yet vulnerable, bairn is already a source of great joy.

The baby's father, Alasdair Geoffrey Ferguson, was named after Geoff Shaw. From conception to birth, Ally mirrored the beginning, gestation, and publication of my biography of the late Gorbals minister-turned-politician. Ally was published as much as he was born. The miniscule debutant yawned through the book launch. Now, 25 years on, he and his partner Sarah have produced our first grandchild.

Like all other children, Danny boy comes to planet Earth with several histories. Sarah's line comes through London and Scotland to Manchester, with social work writ large. The Ferguson tribe originally came from the mining villages of Ayrshire. When the west Fife coal fields opened up in the late 19th century, my grandfather was part of the exodus of those seeking a new living digging the precious "black diamonds" from the dark bowels of the earth. He was one of the people who brought football to Cowdenbeath. From black diamonds to the Blue Brazil.

The history of our clan helps to form who we are, for better or for worse. Sometimes, in order to find life, we have to break away from our histories, but they leave their mark on us. The manner in which family stories are narrated also helps to give us our own place in history. Singular though we may be, we each carry a tribe within us.

It is paradoxical that even as the extended family has given way to the nuclear family which is, in turn, giving way to the atomised family, our obsession with roots grows. The internet websites which help people trace their family lineage are among the busiest on the world wide web.

Up here in Orkney, the burgeoning tourist trade thrives on people from all over the world searching out dark as well as joyful tales of their Orcadian forbears. Orkney's greatest export has been its seafaring adventurers. Innuit adults with names like Flett and Firth make the return arc homeward to find out where their ancestors lived. The past may be another country, but an awful lot of people want to visit it.

In the beginning was the story. For most human beings, relationships and families are what make for happiness and misery, much more so than the passing headlines of the day. The entry of a grandbaby into a troubled yet still enchanting world is a source of great delight. The hope is that the grace-filled story will continue.

There are no guarantees. As time goes on, you become more and more aware of the fragility of everything that lives. Not even fertility is a given. Our life is a promenade theatre of contingency, in which death lurks in the wings, ready to bring down the curtain before the last calls can be taken. Grandchildren are flesh-and-blood bearers of the primeval promise, the seed of immortality. They are much-loved embodiments of the unquenchable human dream.

Tribal dreamings can manifest themselves in less metaphysical, more absurd ways. In two weeks time, another member of the Ferguson tribe will make his debut – for Cowdenbeath Football Club. He is one Ronald Ferguson, son of Joseph, father of Alasdair Geoffrey, and grandfather of Daniel Joseph David. Yes, the electronic crofter will wear the Blue Brazil colours.

No, this is not a spoof. Cowdenbeath are coming up to Orkney to play a pre-season warm-up game, and on Saturday17th July yours truly will take the field for the Blue Brazil against the Orkney Select.

I've always dreamed of playing for Cowdenbeath. At Beath High School, it was only teacher favouritism which prevented me wearing the No 11 jersey, which went unfathomably, to a youngster who was even skinnier than me. His name was Jim Baxter.

But skill cannot be thwarted forever. So now, this late-maturing product of the Cowdenbeath FC youth development programme will take the field, as a substitute, for local charity.

Ever since I've told friends about my upcoming Blue Brazil debut, I've been treated to a litany of disaster stories about people who played fitba when they were old enough to know better. I've heard of everything from severe cramp to spectacular death. I hope to stay near the cramp end of the spectrum.

Still in dreamtime: if I should score a goal, I'll dedicate it to one Daniel Joseph David Ferguson. To become a grandfather and to play for the mighty Blue Brazil feels like immortality to me. Whether there is a wider immortality beyond this seemingly haphazard

44

mortal existence, where the volatile human story comes to an unpredictable but satisfying conclusion, is entirely in the gift of a holy Other. Right now, I'll settle for this little piece of eternity.

We are a grandfather. We are a Cowdenbeath player. We are chuffed.

Bonkle on the brink

I t used to be the prerogative of middle-aged men and women. The quiet, respectable man with the paunch and the wisps of hair which he parted round about his oxters would suddenly shave his head, buy trendy gear, jump on a gleaming new Harley Davidson and roar out of town with a young blonde on the pillion. The woman with the burgeoning hips would start working out at the gym in the latest designer gear, undergo a Botox, get herself a handsome toyboy and head for Patagonia to write her first novel.

The midlife crisis is well documented, and is showing in a street near you. It may not manifest itself in the extreme ways outlined above, but there is a running theme of despair and reinvention. Some of it is common sense, some of it is simply comic. There is nothing more preposterous than middle-aged men pouring their less than svelte bodies into skin-tight gear in order to go out clubbing. And there are few things more embarrassing for kids than to witness their mums, with facial muscles so frozen that they look like the living dead, shaking their silicone-laden breasts to Franz Ferdinand at the local den of iniquity.

It used to be that people were reticent about their age. "I refuse to admit that I am more than 52," said Nancy Astor, "even if that does make my sons illegitimate." Nowadays, it's only the middle-aged who hide their age. Cosmetic surgery can turn mutton into slightly arthritic lamb with cellulite.

In the old days, people didn't live long enough to have a middle-age crisis. They didn't have time, anyway – they were out toiling in the fields 18 hours a day, or giving birth. Scrabbling the earth in the noonday sun without Factor 35 made even 25-year-olds look like George Burns or Naomi Mitchison. Predictions of future facelifts and boob jobs would have had the horny-handed sons and daughters of the soil rolling around, screaming with laughter. Those were the days.

Nowadays, in every town and village in Scotland, the imminence of the age of 45 brings outbreaks of fear and trembling. As you read these wise words – even in places like Bonkle and Kilconquhar – scenes of dark Kierkegaardian angst are being enacted. Gaudy ties are being purchased. Sexual identities are being traded in. Sporty cars are being viewed. Viagra is being ordered online. Desperation is everywhere.

What's all this about? Well, in middle age, the repressed question "Is this it?" bursts into the foreground and demands an answer. Intimations of mortality make urgent the questions about quality, rather than quantity, of life. Have I wasted my life? What are the things I need/would like to do before I hand in my clogs? The brooding Mr Kierkegaard may not be acknowledged, but his questions fill the air.

But there's more. This noble column with its lug to the cultural ground on your behalf, can report tremors. A new phenomenon has appeared. It's called the "quarter-life crisis." I jest not. Many high-flying young

47

people are hitting the existential wall. The approach of the age of 30, it seems, is causing spasms.

New research has shown that some of the country's most talented graduates who were fast-tracked into glittering careers have hit a quarter-life crisis. Bogged down with debt and disillusioned with their jobs, the latest generation of professionals has become desperate to jump off the career ladder. The study has found that eight out of ten successful young people are deep in the throes of a crisis by the time they are in their late twenties.

These are the young people who, disillusioned by age 29, want to scrabble the earth, ride a Harley Davidson round the world, or hive off to Patagonia to write the novel. Angst is coming earlier and earlier, hardly more than a decade after the teenage crisis. If twenty-something soul-searching meets parental midlife crisis, then even Bonkle is on the brink.

How many life crises can one human being take? Some Herald readers are pretty sure there is also a two-thirds life crisis. After my revelation last week that I'm about to make my debut for Cowdenbeath Football Club against Orkney, concerned readers sent gracious, yet horrified, messages telling me it was madness to play. I am touched, so to speak. They wrote in the kindly, solicitous tones used by earnest counselors when dealing with demented clients. I was treated to yet more horror stories about people playing football when past their first flush of youth. A senior editor at the Herald told me about his experience: he hurled himself at a goalmouth cross, missed the ball, crashed into the goal post and broke his nose. Thanks for that.

I am unpersuadable. Today I proudly collected – free, from a local sports shop which is among those sponsoring me for Orkney disability charities – my new football boots, shinguards and jockstrap. It's good to have that support. And surely the monster Orkney defenders won't harm a wee Cowdenbeath guy with specs. Crisis? What two-thirds life crisis?

Blue-rinse dreams and Banoffee pie

BLUE-RINSE DREAMS
AND BANOFFEE PIE
RON FERGUSON

FIFE
SERVI

Foreword by Ian Rankin

Dreams are weird things. One morning, I woke up with a message burning in my brain. I knew that some of the great biblical prophets, like Isaiah and Ezekiel, had woken with a start, suddenly aware that God had been speaking to them. And in modern times, the great Martin Luther King convulsed racist America with his electrifying "I have a dream" oration.

So was this an Orcadian word from the Lord? Two words, in fact – "Banoffee pie". I pondered the deeper meaning of this exotic communication about a pie made with bananas, toffee and cream. Nothing. To this day, I have still not cracked the code.

Compared to flaming visions of heavenly cherubim, or of a land where little black boys and white girls will walk hand in hand, a dream about Banoffee pie lacks a little something. I have been forced to recognise that I am not playing in the premier league of seers and visionaries. More the basement of the third division.

Which brings me, unaccountably, to Cowdenbeath Football Club. My other third division dream came true on Saturday – we all have our ambitions – when the Blue Brazil visited Orkney. I was part of the team, listed in the official programme as a "trialist".

I almost didn't make it. While I was training a few days previously, a group of local lads started a kick-about. It was too good an opportunity to miss. The young men were used to wee boys asking them for a game, but a request from an auld geezer in a Cowdenbeath strip freaked them out. It was great fun until I over-zealously stretched for the ball, and felt my thigh go. When I got home, I could only get up the stairs of the electronic croft with difficulty.

A torn muscle was diagnosed. Having publicly committed myself in the Herald to play, and having got sponsorship for two local disability charities – would I be a visual aid? – this was not good news. However, ultrasound physiotherapy on my wounded leg – one nurse suggested brain surgery might be more appropriate – got me back into shape. In truth, a leg break wouldn't have kept me off the park.

In the half-time tactics talk, the Cowden manager, former Hibs and Scotland striker Keith Wright, told the lads that he wanted to use my awesome pace to unsettle the tiring Orkney defence. When I did come on, 15 minutes from the end, it was a fantastic thrill to play for the club I've loved since childhood.

I had dyed my hair blue for the occasion – it's payback time when you can embarrass your kids – and the rain threatened to turn my face into a grotesque version of Braveheart. The bigger worry was that I would be scythed by a gorilla from Stromness, some huge Orcadian farmer used to carrying a bull under each oxter.

If I'd retaliated, I could have become a new religious icon – Saint Off. The banter was brilliant. After I managed to put the ball between the legs of one defender, the poor guy got endless stick from his peers about having been nutmegged by the oldest man in Orkney.

Cowdenbeath have the youngest team in Scottish senior football. I was partnered up front by a brilliant 16-year-old trialist, Craig Scott, who signed a two-year contract after the game. He obviously thought he'd be playing alongside me every week. These young guys have their own dreams of making a name in the game, and good luck to them.

I can recommend living the dream, whether lofty or lowly. Life is too short to waste on boring routines. It's never too late to tear up the script. Look at President George Bush, senior. To celebrate his 80th birthday, he went skydiving. (Pity he hadn't been holding his beloved son, and dropped the bugger on top of a self-satisfied Tony Blair as he sunned himself in a deckchair.)

It's never too late to climb that mountain or write that novel, or even that little book of family stories for your grandchildren. Nor is it ever too soon to dream the dream. It may be to find a cure for cancer or to be a good parent, to climb Kilimanjaro or to play hockey for Ecclefechan, to be a missionary-explorer in darkest Wick or to help a disabled child to smile. To fail to make the dream come true is not a sin; to fail to try is.

The Blue Brazil number 11 jersey, a generous gift from the club, is on my study wall as I write. It reminds me of another number 11 from Cowdenbeath, the late, great, Jim Baxter who, despite his own mortal frailties, showed us how the beautiful game should be played.

One day I'll tell my new and gorgeous grandson, Daniel, about Slim Jim; and also about how his own, crazed, blue-haired grandfather once helped the mighty Blue Brazil to win 9-1 in Orkney. And I'll quiz Daniel about his own dreams – perhaps about taking on lions in dens – and about the hidden meaning of Banoffee pie.

The new electronic tagging

The paramedics who rushed to the scene at Queen Street station were astounded to see someone trying to resuscitate the shabby old victim by breathing into an orifice well south of his mouth. Why was he doing that? "Well, you should try smelling his breath," came the rejoinder.

This grotesque tale came to mind with the news that a German telecommunications company is developing the first mobile phone that will alert users when their breath is bad or if they are giving off offensive smells. The phone will use a tiny chip to detect unpleasant odours. "It examines the air in the immediate vicinity for anything from bad breath and alcohol to atmospheric gas levels," said a fragrant, serious, spokeswoman for Siemens Mobile.

So if you see a businessman holding his mobile close to his underarm, it's not because he's developed a talking oxter. The beeping noise will tell him that he may not make the impression at the sales conference he desires.

The mobile phone has revolutionized our lives. There are now more mobiles in Britain than there are people. What is surprising is that the latest surge in sales is not among teenagers, but pensioners. The top-speed texter sitting next to you on the bus may be an arthritic greatgrandmother putting a bet on.

The pocket phone has come a long way very quickly. Launched for business executives about 20 years ago, the early versions were like electronic bricks. You could tell the owners by their lopsided Monty Python walks. The potential for expansion in cash-rich Britain was obvious, and gobsmacked punters, who hadn't quite grasped the concept, were soon asking their pals how their wives knew they were in the pub.

Developments in microtechnology, driven by the overflowing pots of gold at the end of that particular rainbow, rapidly delivered the miniscule handsets which have turned most people in this country into walking transmitters.

This is where the problems begin. A walking transmitter is a potential walking pest. The very advantages of mobile technology – instant communication to and from just about anywhere in the globe – are what makes the portable wireless phone such a menace. Exasperated Oscar-winning actor Kevin Spacey this week felt compelled to warn his audiences at the Old Vic to stay at home if they can't control their mobiles.

Cinemas, funerals, weddings and public meetings are not complete without the dreaded ringtones, or those annoying beeps from a text message which start an epidemic of distracting fumbling.

Travelling by train to avoid the strain is a thing of the past. The once-pleasurable rail journey has turned into a nightmare on wheels. Every carriage is like a BT exchange. What is even worse than the incessant intrusive ringing are the one-sided calls of stupefying banality. These are the main evidence that radiation from mobile phones causes brain death.

Being able to be contacted any time, anywhere, has a terrible downside. There is no escape from a demanding employer. The omnipresent mobile means that even though you're on holiday at the uttermost ends of the earth, your baleful boss is only a nano-second away. It's a form of electronic tagging. Big Brother is in your jacket pocket or handbag, and if you answer his summons with a hint of drink on your breath, an alarm will no doubt go off. Charles Kennedy, be afraid, be very afraid, even in your highland croft.

Technology is not neutral. The invention of the stirrup transformed medieval warfare. The making of clocks radically changed our attitudes to time and efficiency. The mobile phone is transforming the way we work, in many cases doing away with the need for an office.

That tiny phone is a games machine, an address book, a clock, an alarm, a music maker, and an instant transmitter of photographs. It brings ever-new opportunities to spend our money. People now download about twice as many pop chart ringtones as they buy CD singles. The next generation of phones will offer high-speed data transmission, including the ability to make video calls where you can see the other person, and download movie clips and music.

There are now about 1.4 billion mobile phones in the world – far more than there are computers, and about 100 million more than there are television sets. This is the fastest-growing technology the world has ever seen. Britain is throwing out more than 1m tonnes of electronic "e-waste", including discarded mobile phones, every year.

What is lagging behind the smart technology is an etiquette and a set of ethics. This tiny device which can take communication opportunities to a new level, afford high-tech personal safety, extend the reach of an employer's control, allow governments to instant-message reluctant citizens, and detonate a terrorist bomb, is a joy and a curse. And with your personalised ringtone, you need ask not for whom the bell tolls.

Now your phone can even do an oxter sniff – yours and your close neighbour's. With that one device, you can both call out the paramedics and check the air quality. It's a wonderful thing, progress.

Time to ban this steamy book!

I t's surely time for Christians to call for the banning of a controversial international best-selling book which is full of tales of violence, rape, polygamy, ethnic cleansing, scheming ambition, adultery, and foul murder. The book's main hero, who doesn't make his appearance till late on in the drama, undermines the traditional idea of the family. Such is the book's reputation that there is no need even to read it before taking to the streets in protest. The name of the seditious tome is the Holy Bible.

More than 47,000 people wrote or phoned the BBC to protest about its intention to screen *Jerry Springer – The Opera* last Saturday night. The critics claimed that the musical featured more than 8000 swear words, as well as lampooning Jesus Christ. A protest group, Christian Voice, published telephone numbers of BBC executives on the internet, sparking abusive calls and threats of violence. The group now intends to sue the BBC for blasphemy.

I want to move the debate on a bit, but first it's worth looking at some of the facts about the show which is currently wowing them in London's West End. The musical is a gleefully offensive send-up of the record-breaking American TV chat show, in which Jerry

Springer hosts confessions, brawls and slanging-matches among guests chosen for their low-life behaviour and attitudes.

In the musical, Springer gets to interrogate Satan, Christ, Adam and Eve, the Virgin Mary and God about who is really to blame for the mess of the world. In the resulting row God wryly sings, "It Ain't Easy to Be Me." Springer absolves himself of the chaos he creates, backing his mantra "I don't solve problems, I just televise them" with the claim "There is no wrong or right. Everything is holy." In other words, the musical takes the amoral values of the *Jerry Springer Show* to their logical conclusion and satirises them. Surely that isn't too difficult a Christian concept?

It turns out that the figure of 8000 obscenities was arrived at by multiplying the number of swear words by the number of people singing them in the show, including the 27-strong chorus. Hey, this is Christian mathematics! Here are some more facts. Christian Voice, which portrays those who disagree with its views as "enemies of God", also fulminates against the European Union, the legality of homosexuality and the abolition of the death penalty. Its director, Stephen Green, is on record as advocating the quarantining of people living with HIV and AIDS, and the withdrawal of public funding from groups supporting them. Such a nice Christian chap.

Tory deputy leader Michael Ancram joined in the Springer criticism. "You can choose to go to the theatre, that is where you go to see freedom of expression," he said solemnly. "Public service television, I believe, has another duty and that is to exercise a degree of caution."

Eh? And here was me thinking that all television sets were fitted with an off-switch.

59

I don't want to be saved from adult choices by zealots who want to do a bit of censoring or hand-chopping on God's behalf. The BBC recently dropped a cartoon satire, *Popetown*, after more than 6,000 Roman Catholics complained before they had seen it. One prominent Catholic even threatened to top himself if the show went ahead. Sikh protestors managed to stop the play Behzti in Birmingham after violent protests and threats against its Sikh writer. Many of those who burned their television licences in public argued that the BBC wouldn't dare satirise the prophet Muhammad. If so, more's the pity. Muslim bullies are no better than Christian bullies, and they need to be stood up to.

It is now argued that the blasphemy laws, which are in place to protect the Christian God, should be extended to all religions. God forbid. The blasphemy laws should be swept from the statute books without delay. For Christ's sake, is the deity really so weak that he needs to be defended by obnoxious creeps with a humour-bypass like Stephen Green? Not in my name, pal.

Satire and iconoclasm have always had an honourable place within the Christian tradition. Not only the biblical prophets, but brilliants like Jonathan Swift and Soren Kierkegaard – even that late, lamented Kirk elder Ricky Fulton – have used devastating satire in the interest of truth.

Christianity has had a privileged position for far too long. Religious adherents need to make their case in today's market place of ideas by the integrity of their thinking and the attractiveness of their exemplars and not by blasphemy laws, historic privileges, threats, serial taking of offence and fatwas.

Ironically, the venomous protests have had the effect of increasing ticket sales for the Springer musical.

London's Cambridge Theatre is now offering a discount to people carrying Bibles to the musical, enabling them to get in for just £10. Now that's what I call style – especially since these same scriptures contain steamy scenes which, if translated to the small screen, could not be shown before the watershed.

Transport of delight

O h, what transport of delight! Travelling in Prague last week was a joy. Yes, a joy. Try substituting Glasgow for Prague in that sentence, and the whole thing immediately becomes risible. Even walking around the midden which is Glasgow – up to your oxters in greasy fish supper wrappings, clanking beer cans and garish pizza boxes – is a trial, never mind trying to get on one of the filthy buses.

Glasgow is simply an extreme example. Edinburgh may be fur coats and nae knickers; Glasgow has knickers but they haven't been changed for months. Our cities would be shortlisted for any European City of Filth competition; they would also be contenders for the world transport shambles championship.

This is a glaring Scottish problem, but it only becomes truly glaring when you travel elsewhere. Why am I rhapsodising about Prague? Because you can travel around a clean, beautiful city in easeful comfort, whether on foot or by tram, bus or subway. Has this happened because the Czech Republic is crammed with specialists in rocket science? No. The transporting of people around a clean city – and Prague has nearly twice the population of Glasgow – does not present insurmountable challenges to the human mind at the beginning of the 21st century.

Here is what happens in Prague. You buy a ticket at any newsagents at any time. The same ticket is valid for bus, tram and metro. The ticket isn't activated and time-stamped until you insert it into a simple machine at the metro or on the bus or tram. You only have to do it once.

The times of the plentiful buses, trams and subway cars are posted everywhere and – miracle of miracles – they mean what they say. The good citizens of Prague would be furious if they had to wait more than ten minutes. I'm not kidding. Because public transport is so reliable and comfortable, few people bring their car into the city. Why on earth should they?

Compare and contrast the City of Culture. In Glasgow recently I felt embarrassed on behalf of some Japanese visitors who made the mistake of trying to travel by bus. The notice at the bus stop declared that they had to have the right fare – but they didn't know what the right fare was. Gotcha, you buggers! That'll teach you for being foreign! When they struggled on to the bus, they encountered a snarling driver. They didn't have the right money, so they ended up paying over the odds. Once they were inside, they realised they were travelling in a manky tip on wheels. Welcome to bonnie Scotland.

It is crazy to have people queuing up to buy tickets from the person who is actually driving the bus. The vehicle cannot move until the driver has sorted out all the problems. When he does eventually lurch off, the streets are clogged with cars, driven by people who won't leave their vehicle at home. Why? Because public transport is so bad.

On my return to Orkney, I discovered that Northlink Ferries have changed their timetable after minimalist "consultation" with the bus and rail operators. This means that Orcadian punters, after cheerily bouncing over the Pentland Firth for nearly two hours, may face a two or three hour wait before boarding a bus or train for an interminable journey down to the central belt. Anybody who wants a taster of eternity should try this journey. The wheels on the bus go round and round, all day long.

Surely it doesn't require a Third Reich to get a decent transport system? We are governed by numbskulls who have run out of excuses. People complain that the Scottish Executive doesn't have enough of the "vision thingie", as Prince Charles would put it so eloquently. Listen, I don't want a "visionary" Jack McConnell. The very idea is enough to keep me awake at night. I want a government which will manage competently the things which need to be done to make public life tolerable, and then get out of my life.

We don't need more think tanks or huge consultants' fees. Here, for free, is the answer. Firstly, get Jack the lad on to Prague buses. Secondly, determine to spend ten per cent of what our involvement in Iraq has cost us, to get a decent transport system under way. Thirdly, reverse the de-regulation nonsense which means the ordinary punter hasn't a clue who's running what, when. Fourthly, appoint a national Transport Thug with powers to bang the heads of the ferry, rail and bus authorities together until they cry for mercy and produce an integrated timetable. Fifthly, institute a reign of terror against anybody who drops rubbish on the street or on public transport.

When that's done, it will be a pleasure to travel around our beautiful country. The emissions of poisonous pollutants will be greatly reduced. We'll travel quickly across our cities. Tourists will be able to appreciate our wonderful buildings without wading through dogshit and detritus. A Prague Spring will be followed by a Scottish winter wonderland. The revolution starts now.

Adoration of the Maggie

So it was the Lord wot done it. Yahweh apparently brought together a wonderful, wonderful couple, and made them happy. It is the love story of our time, a sweeping, "Gone with the Wind" epic, crossing continents and time zones. It features a square-jawed, handsome hero and a swooning lady with a handbag. Ronnie and Maggie. Maggie and Ronnie. Fighting evil. Together forever. It is a tale which has made millions weep. We'll come back to it in a minute.

When President George Bush, sen, was fighting a war or something, and was too busy to attend the funeral of General Charles de Gaul, he despatched three former US presidents – Gerald Ford, Jimmy Carter, and Richard Nixon – to represent him. When the image of the three men, standing on the stairway up to the aircraft, appeared in the American media, Bob Dole memorably described the scene as "Hear no evil", "See no evil", and "Evil".

For some reason, American presidents are perpetually entangled with evil. Apocalyptic language seems to go with the office. The enemy is always unequivocally satanic. There are white hats and black hats. There are sheriffs whose job is to kick evil ass all over town. And when the American sheriffs have equally

66

messianic British deputy-dawgs, the crusading mentality goes into overdrive. To ask questions about a precipitate rush to sort out the "axis of evil", for instance, is to be guilty of betrayal of goodness, of God even. Self-doubt must be allowed no entry point. A bending of the truth is not a crime when it's the Lord's business.

Ronald Reagan had his "evil empire". In the western which played out perpetually in his filmy mind, this amiable, lazy, sheriff represented righteousness, pure and simple. The laziness – which caused Gore Vidal to dub the former movie performer "The Acting President" – was a mercy. It was once said of Reagan that a particular crisis had given the President "many a sleepless afternoon". Most people only felt secure when the Chief of Staff was asleep.

The partnership between the comatose sheriff and the messianic harridan with the overactive political thyroid was a truly remarkable one. While Ronnie dozed in the afternoons, Maggie stalked the earth, swinging her handbag. At night, when the Gipper was even more deeply in the land of Nod, Boadicea was prowling about on our behalf. She manically exulted in this unnatural capacity. Like the God with whom she increasingly confused herself, she neither slumbered nor slept.

This week, we were given a revealing glimpse into the Adoration of the Maggie, with the publication of Reagan: A Life in Letters, consisting of newly-found draft letters to fellow world statesmen and family Americans.

"Throughout my life," Ronnie wrote breathlessly to Maggie in 1994, "I've always believed that life's path is determined by a Force more powerful than fate. I feel the Lord has brought us together for a profound purpose, and that I have been richly blessed for having known you."

Michty me! I hear the scraping of violins. Did the fragrant Maggie blush when she read it? One feels proud to have lived on earth at the same time as this star-crossed duo. Has there ever been such a relationship since Anthony and Cleopatra, or Abelard and Heloise? Or John and Edwina? The epistle goes on:

"I am proud to call you one of my dearest friends, Margaret; proud to have shared many of life's significant moments with you, and thankful that God brought you into my life. Sincerely, Ron"

Please, please, no more! This is unbearably beautiful. Unbearable, anyway. You could hardly make this stuff up. Well, you could, actually. Grateful hacks get paid bawbees for churning this stuff out for B-movies. In fact, Big Ron may have been repeating a line from the movie he shared with Bonzo the monkey before he successfully auditioned for the role of a bumbling "Aw shucks" president.

I know that you cannot cope with any more emotional intensity, but I must close with a couple of quotes from a letters cache I found in a listless barrel on the Pentland Firth. The first is from a man called Tony. It's addressed to someone he clearly looks up to.

"Dear George, you have always been a shining hero to me, a colossus bestriding the earth. I feel that the Lord has brought us together for the benefit of all humankind. I believe that the sun and moon and stars shine out of your arsenal. Look, I am proud to be your devoted servant, to follow wherever thou dost lead. P.S. If you need any double-glazing done at the White House, just give me five minutes with your people and I'll persuade them! Yours in Christ, Tone."

The second is actually an email. It seems to be addressed to the same Tony. Because it's marked "strictly confidential" I will conceal the writer's identity writer, simply calling him A******r C******l. It simply says:

"Hi mate. I think we're f****d."

Compared to Ronnie and Tony's effusions, it lacks a certain charm, don't you think? Its only strength is that it tells it like it is.

The Grapes of wrath gave Luther Gyp

The seat of the Reformation has been unearthed – and it turns out to be a toilet seat. German archaeologists have discovered the toilet on which some historians believe Martin Luther wrote the famous 95 Theses that launched the Protestant Reformation. The 16th century Augustinian monk, Catholic priest and university professor is the historical Godfather of evangelical Christianity, which is the focus of so much attention today.

Historians have averred for years that the Protestant Reformation's founding father wrote his revolutionary theses while on *das klo*, as the Germans call it. But they did not know where the object was until archaeologists discovered the stone building after stumbling across the remains of an annexe of his home in Wittenberg, south-west of Berlin.

"This is a great find," Professor Stefan Rhein, director of the Luther Memorial Foundation said, "particularly because we're talking about someone whose texts we have concentrated on for years, while little attention has been paid to anything three-dimensional and human behind them. This is where the birth of the Reformation took place. Luther said himself that he made his reformatory discovery in *cloaca* (Latin for sewer). We just had no idea where this sewer was. Now it's clear what the Reformer meant."

The 450-year-old lavatory, which was very advanced for its time, is made out of stone blocks and, unusually, has a 30cm-square seat with a hole. Underneath is a cesspit attached to a primitive drain. Father Luther frequently alluded to the fact that he suffered from chronic constipation and that he spent much of his time in contemplation on the lavatory.

Question: would the Reformation have happened if Luther had not been so anally retentive? Picture, if you will, a frustrated and furious German monk – think Berti Vogts in drag – straining in das kludgie. His haemorrhoids – the grapes of wrath? – are giving him gyp. As he feverishly scribbles a series of controversial theses, he is worried not just about his troublesome bowels, but his eternal salvation. The screwed-up face of this troubled monk will fail to launch a thousand shits but will set in motion a theological and ecclesiastical revolution which will change Europe for ever.

Luther's angstful problem was this: how can a sinful human being ever justify his life before a holy God? He went to confession almost every day, sometimes for up to six hours, going over his sins, both real and imagined. At one point an exasperated confessor told him to go and commit a really spectacular sin, rather than keep coming back with miniscule peccadilloes. "Man, God is not angry with you, you are angry with God," he told Luther.

How could he be sure that he had truly confessed all his sins? And how could he be certain he had eternal life? The Catholic Church, which claimed to control such access in the name of God, had become so corrupt that it sold indulgences to parishioners, assuring them that the minute they handed over the cash they could ill

71

afford, their dead relatives would move up a few grades in purgatory. Luther exploded in rage against his Church's mercenary exploitation of people's insecurities.

How was his problem resolved for him? Luther explained it in his brilliant lectures on Saint Paul at the University of Wittenburg, where he was by then professor of biblical studies. "Then I grasped that the justice of God is that righteousness by which through grace and sheer mercy God justifies us through faith. Thereupon I felt myself to be reborn and to have gone through an open door into paradise."

Jesus took away Luther's sins but left him with his haemorrhoids. Ach well. The obstinate, articulate theologian collided with complacent Vatican officials who were too arrogant to bother to read the disturbing European runes. Luther's magnificent translation of the Bible, pouring from Gutenberg's presses, captured the popular imagination. The rest is turbulent history.

Today's evangelical Christians would actually be very uncomfortable with the flesh-and-blood Luther. No proto-Puritan, he was as bawdy as he was brilliant, and his language was scatological. In an impolite time, faecal language was often used to denigrate the devil, such as Luther's "I shit on the devil". This was probably wishful thinking on the part of a constipated man.

Meanwhile, back at the toilet. Professor Rhein has promised that his foundation would prevent the 80,000 visitors who arrive in Wittenberg each year in search of the spirit of Luther, from sitting on the sacred lavvy. "I would not sit on it. There's a point where you have to draw the line," he said. The bottom line. You might catch more than you think.

Fast forward to a 21st century luxurious toilet, where one of Luther's children, an anal-retentive president, sits with his breeks round his ankles, scribbling notes. Had it not been for the 16th century Reformer, he might have still been drunkenly propping up a Texas bar. With all the zeal of a convert, he is plotting more fire upon the earth. Note: never underestimate people who make their plans on the potty.

Shooting the messenger

T he dilapidated 18th century mansion stands against the backdrop of a stunning landscape and seascape, several hundred yards from where I live. The Georgian house was once the grandest country house in mainland Orkney. Now, a campaign has been launched to restore the house, and – just as important – to restore the reputation of its most famous occupant. This is a tale of heroic adventure, cover-up, upper-class skulduggery, and cannibalism.

The crumbling, yet still beautiful, Hall of Clestrain was featured in the first programme of the new series of Restoration on BBC2 on Tuesday evening. The mansion was built in 1769 by upwardly mobile Orcadian merchant, Patrick Honeyman. The next generation moved their base to central Scotland, leaving their estate factor, John Rae and his wife, to live in and look after the house.

It is the Raes' fourth son, John, born in 1813, who is the focus of our interest. Like most young Orcadians of his day, he became skilled as a seaman and a hunter. After qualifying as a doctor, he also followed the path of many Orcadians by joining the Hudson Bay Company. Beginning as a surgeon aboard the Prince of Wales, bound for the North Atlantic and the Arctic, he explored and mapped more of Canada than any other human being, and made his reputation as one of the greatest ever Arctic explorers.

Rae's tactic was to learn the skills of the Inuit and the Cree Indians. In London's class-ridden upper echelons, the independent-minded Orcadian was accused of going native, rather than imposing British customs upon the Esquimaux. Charles Dickens wrote unequivocally: "We believe every savage to be in his heart covetous, treacherous, and cruel." Unlike the noble Brits.

The British establishment's favourite explorer was Sir John Franklin, who had set out with 100 men in 1845 on a Royal Navy Expedition to discover the Northwest Passage. After the expedition went missing, a huge rescue operation was launched under the leadership of Sir John Richardson and the indispensable Dr John Rae. The expedition turned up few clues to the fate of Franklin. Rae stayed on, and continued to survey over a thousand miles of uncharted coastline. He also discovered the last uncharted link in the Northwest Passage, succeeding where Franklin had failed.

Now this is where it gets really interesting. What the Restoration programme didn't report was that Rae, who was much respected by the Inuit people, learned from his contacts that some time previously, Inuit hunters had discovered bodies and graves of Europeans, as well as artifacts belonging to the Franklin expedition. The artifacts, some of which Rae bought, included kettles which had been used for the boiling of human flesh.

It is fascinating to read John Rae's sober account, written in 1854. "From the mutilated state of many of the bodies and the contents of the kettles, it is evident that our wretched countrymen had been driven to the last dread alternative – cannibalism – as a means of prolonging existence."

The conclusion caused fury at the Admiralty in London. Lady Franklin was spitting blood, demanding vengeance against the man who had dared to suggest such a dastardly thing. Charles Dickens leapt to the defence of the lady, dismissing "the chatter of a gross handful of uncivilized people, with a domesticity of blood and blubber".

Victorian London was scandalised. The immediate verdict in the clubs was that no Englishman would ever resort to eating the flesh of another Englishman, not even in extremis. The message was unthinkable: therefore, the messenger would have to be shot. Rather than being decorated, Rae was airbrushed out of history. His name was removed from the records. Angered by this injustice, Orcadians had a statue of their local hero erected by public subscription and placed in St Magnus Cathedral.

In the 1980s and early 1990s, anthropologists recovered the permafrosted remains of some of Franklin's men. There was evidence that the bodies had been cut up and the flesh removed from the bones. The scientists concluded that cannibalism was the likely cause.

At a time when the honours system is due to be reformed is also appropriate to reflect on those who were unjustly dishonoured: the whistleblowers, the bearers of unacceptable tidings, those who challenged the deeply held assumptions of their day.

And one does not have to be a conspiracy theorist to raise questions about the pin-striped, clubby, assumptions of the Huttons and Butlers of our land. Britain may be less class-ridden than it once was, but tides of apparent reasonableness can still swamp sharp questions about public accountability. Nor is it improper to wonder aloud when a judge who downloads pornographic pictures of little boys into his computer escapes the custodial fate of lesser mortals. Proper Englishmen of a certain stripe may still lead charmed lives, while the ladies of these lords spit blood and demand heads on platters.

A handsome, silent, crumbling building, shaken by severe Orkney gales, raises eloquent questions about power, privilege, influence, the treatment of "inferior" peoples, and vicious spindoctoring. The answers, my friends, are blowing in the wind.

Red the Lurcher frees
the prisoners

I t's always reassuring to be surrounded by dumb
animals. Any creature which is both dumber than
you and utterly loyal to you is a joy and a treasure.
My dog, Bess, makes your electronic crofter feel like a
veritable Einstein. On matters to do with Kierkegaard,
for instance, she defers to my superior knowledge.

But what if the dumb animals are not so dumb?
What if they are actually fooling their so-called superiors
in order to gain free bread and board? Suddenly, the
secure structure of our world comes crashing down.
What if Bess actually knows more about Kierkegaard
than I do, but strings me along because the biscuits are
good?

What has prompted these disturbing musings is the
astonishing performance of Red the lurcher. Staff at the
Battersea Dogs' Home were baffled when, for several
mornings in a row, they arrived for work to find some of
the dogs had escaped and wreaked havoc in the
kitchens. Determined to find the culprit, managers
installed video cameras. As they looked at the film, the
staff saw a single figure slide back the steel bolt in Red's
cage, tug open the door and slip out. Glancing about to
avoid the night-time security, he then moved quickly
from kennel to kennel to free other dogs.

What astonished the managers was that the culprit was not a cat-burglar, so to speak, but a dog. Yes, Red the Lurcher, rather than Bob the Builder. Four-year-old Red had worked out that by reaching up on his hind paws and using his nose and teeth, he could undo the bolt.

Becky Blackmore, of Battersea Dogs' Home, said: "We would come in to several dogs out on their block. They had had lots of food, lots of fun and games, and caused loads of mess. There are many stories about Battersea being haunted, so we wanted to make sure that there was an explanation for what was going on, and we managed to catch the culprit. It is amazing, really, because lurchers aren't particularly renowned for their intelligence."

Aha! It turns out that lurchers are intelligent dogs pretending to be stupid in order to outwit stupid humans who are pretending to be intelligent. I think that Red has a great career ahead of him as security consultant to Reliance. Scotland is currently overrun with escaped prisoners, but Red would second-guess them any time.

He should also be put immediately in charge of security at the new Scottish Parliament. I wouldn't be surprised if he's been in there already, dressed – given his name – as Tommy Sheridan.

I think that this is the real story of the week. It's much more interesting than the Conservative Party's attempt to make the case for euthanasia by providing a public example of a corporate being which should be put out of its misery.

Red's midnight party is miles more significant than Jack McConnell's Lanarkshire shuffle of dumb animals. I'm convinced that David Blunkett's guide-dog would make a much more intelligent home secretary than her master is.

79

More accumulating evidence: dogs can detect bladder cancer by sniffing urine. That may not seem a great way to spend your day, but if you're a dog, it's fantastic. There are huge machines which cost millions of pounds to detect such things, but a daft wee dug can do the diagnostic business with one sniff. Dumb animals? I tell you, Jack Russells will soon be working as consultants in our understaffed hospitals.

In my days as a meenister before returning to hackery, I used to be amazed at how family pooches would make unerringly for the crotch, as if by some homing mechanism. Let me tell you from experience that it's quite hard to discourse authoritatively about the Holy Trinity while a canine snout is rooting around your genital area in a quite unPresbyterian manner. What I ken now is that Rover was actually on diagnostic business.

Another fascinating story this week concerns a man and his faithful dog. All sensitive males should look away now. Constantin Mocanu, a 67-year-old from a village near the Spanish town of Galati, rushed out into his yard in his underwear to kill a noisy chicken keeping him awake at night.

But instead of cutting the chicken's throat, Mr Mocanu cut off his own penis. Yes.

He said: "I confused it with the chicken's neck. I cut it and the dog rushed and ate it." Man's best friend. The dear soul confused his willy with a chicken neck! Which was the dumb animal here?

Readers will no doubt be grateful for this noble column's unremitting quest to find the meaningful in the midst of the mundane. Speaking of which, the electronic crofter will be at Hampden on Saturday to watch Scotland attempt to play football. If that itself isn't stupid enough, we will eat mince pies the likes of which choosy

80

dogs would refuse, and we will bawl the utterly preposterous Flower of Scotland. And, when I return to Orkney, Bess will eat up her expensive biscuits, and laugh in a knowing, Kierkegaardian, way.

Madonna in Jerusalem

adonna in Jerusalem: it has a certain feel to
it. Yet the lady who sings and swings – crucifix
flying and diamond-studded bodice gleaming –
and then stands at the holy city's Wailing Wall, is no
virgin mother. Not only that, she now announces herself
to the world under the Hebrew name Ha Malkah Esther
– Queen Esther. Meanwhile, back at the supposed site of
the crucifixion of Jesus Christ, monks are brawling and
swapping punches. Welcome to the city of dreams, the
city of nightmares.

Too many riches here. We'll come back to the
monkish rammy in a minute. First, turn the searchlight
on rock's putative queen of heaven swaying at the
Wailing Wall, surrounded by hordes of photographers.
When the pop diva's convoy stopped near Judaism's
holiest site, Orthodox Jews shouted at her to go home.
The material girl, whose wealth outstrips the gross
national product of some Third World countries, was
disinclined to take their advice. After all, wasn't she in
the holy city to study their religion?

Maybe. The agenda was a gathering of about 2,000
followers of Kabbalah, a form of Jewish mysticism. At her
behest the Los Angeles Kabbalah Centre, the wondrous
organization which organised the event, insisted that

reporters covering her visit wear white. Thinking of the grizzled hacks I know, this is a vision of pure delight.

Kabbalah is attracting some seriously rich superstars. So what's it all about? Kabbalah means "received wisdom" in Hebrew. It contains much secret lore. It's an esoteric form of religion, characterized by Gnostic signs and fantastic speculation. Early forms of Kabbalah showed evidence of Egyptian, Persian and then neo-Platonic influence. If you can but crack the secret codes, it will tell you the dates of the end of the world, the timing of the next world war, the fate of Gordon Brown, and Cowdenbeath's football results for the next three years. In these troubled times, it is a pseudo-philosophical field of dreams for hucksters and an irresistible magnet for heidbangers. Welcome to Gullible's Travels.

An American rabbi, Philip Berg, popularized some Kabbalahistic texts in the 1960s, and the New Age-Old Age musings became cult best sellers. If you were going to California, you would wear colours in your hair and carry the texts. Critical of the failed certainties of mainstream religions, credulous seekers then gulped down six hundred impossible things before vegetarian breakfast.

Kabbalah has proved to be the late 20th and early 21st century designer religion of choice for the superstars. As well as Madonna, it draws adherents such as Britney Spears, Demi Moore and Roseanne Barr. The pleasant thing about it is that this kind of religion makes no inconvenient demands about justice for the poor. You don't even have to listen to the howls of the Palestinians as they beat on their own Wailing Wall – the dominating fence that carves through their land.

The Flower of Dornoch herself wears a red cord round her wrist to ward off the evil eye – how long before Cherie gets one to protect herself and her trembling man against their brooding Downing Street neighbour? Madonna's husband, the British film director Guy Ritchie, was seen dancing with a Torah scroll. That surely must be one of the signs of the end of the world.

Fearful that the Kabbalah people might be trying to separate his wife from her money, Ritchie checked them out for himself. His eloquent and elevating verdict? "Put it this way, I've never met a Kabbalahist who is a cunt." Nice bit of religious alliteration, but I suspect he didn't look hard enough.

What is genuinely interesting about all this is that Madonna is the latest in a line of superstars to find that when she eventually got to the top of the career mountain, the view wasn't what was promised on the tin. Many well-heeled travellers have come back from the far country with a similar story. Having sacrificed a private life on the altar of fame, wealth, and celebrity, the end result turns out to be a feeling of emptiness. Hence the quest.

But why the avoidance of mainstream religion? An extreme answer to that question lies at the Church of the Holy Sepulchre in Jerusalem. A punch-up erupted between Greek Orthodox and Franciscan monks during a procession to mark the discovery in 327 by Helena, mother of Constantine, of your actual True Cross. What was it that caused a holy procession to turn into an eye-gouging, kneeing-in-the-groin, Ayrshire juniors football match? Someone left a chapel door open. No kidding. You could not make this stuff up. Only Monty Python could begin to do it justice.

There's an old Celtic saying to the effect that if you go to Jerusalem or Rome to seek God, you'll only find him there if you take him with you in the first place.

Forget esoteric texts, red cords, ubiquitous true crosses and fake "biblical" sites, and avoid hooligan monks. So there's a bit of secret knowledge for you – for which your humble hack in the spotless white suit makes no charge.

Pontius pilate with a ponytail

She swings in the wind from a crane in the main square of the city. After all, she had it coming. The judge who ordered her execution was so incensed by her "sharp tongue" and the insouciant removing of her headscarf in court that he decided a public hanging was necessary. So angry was this zealous preserver of public order that he insisted on putting the noose around her neck himself. A man's gotta do what a man's gotta do.

Thus does 16-year-old Atefeh Rajabi get her just reward, according to Sharia law. She hangs there, *pour encourager les autres*. What was the heinous crime that merited public execution? Having sex before marriage. The same law which provided her death warrant let her lover off with 100 lashes. After all, the male is always less culpable.

The gruesome execution took place last week in the Iranian city of Neka. It confirms the prejudices of every bar-room Islamophobe. Aren't these Muslims barbaric? They don't have our civilised standards, do they? Meanwhile, many multi-culturalists shuffle in an awkward silence, unwilling to speak out. After all, it's not right to condemn other cultures, is it? Everything is relative, don't you agree?

Get real. The execution of a 16-year-old girl for having sex with her boyfriend is an act of unspeakable barbarism, and no equivocation is possible. If our only choice is between an incandescent judge with medieval inclinations and Pontius Pilate with a ponytail, there is no civilised place to go.

We need to start somewhere, so let's go back to that other courtroom in the pub, where Islam is on trial. The accusers at the bar apparently need no knowledge of the majesty of the seminal contributions of Islamic civilisation to the story of the western world, never mind to the eastern narrative. No hints of the richness of the Sufi tradition of spirituality need detain them. They are innocent of any knowledge of sophisticated Islamic philosophy or mathematics or science or architecture or art, or of the charitable practices of millions of Muslims throughout the world. Why should such considerations trouble their beer-gutted certainties, especially when they have such an erudite spokesman as the fragrant Robert Kilroy-Silk, who can assure them that all these dodgy hand-chopping, eye-gouging Arabs have contributed nothing of interest to human life as we know it, Jim?

Meanwhile, on the left field, seated like a tableau of Rodin's Thinkers, the members of the discussion group avert their eyes from the figure dancing grotesquely in the wind, and whisper that since everything is relative, who are they to judge other cultures? Anyway, everything's the fault of the Americans. Yes, it's all right to judge and blame the Yanks.

Behind these scenes lies a fundamental question: how are we to live with each other on this fragile planet? Gross stereotyping, glaring economic injustice, and the availability of the technology of mass slaughter will be the death of our children's children, if not of us. The stakes are very, very high.

87

Nothing less than a change in human consciousness will do. What we badly lack is a sense of critical solidarity with all humanity. Solidarity, in the biblical sense of seeing all human beings as God-bearers, or however else we want to frame the awesome reality of sentient humanity. Critical, in that a generous celebration of the many forms of human life doesn't mean that we have to leave our brains at the door of the sanctuary.

Sending a child to the gallows for having sex is barbarism. End of story. Not to protest such acts is to collude. There is no water-filled basin which will free us from a ultimate judgment at the bar of history, never mind heaven. Here-and-now truthfulness demands a private and public critique of certain aspects of Islam, in solidarity with Muslims who are already making that critique themselves. It also necessitates the discipline of understanding Islam in all its richness, and not accepting some grotesque tabloidised caricature.

There is a problem for "us", though. The postmodern philosophers are partially right. The Enlightenment, which enthroned a scientific, rationalist view of the world, presumed that "our" rationality was the gold standard. This was one of the arrogant assumptions which, linked with the then high-tech ships and armaments, fuelled the colonisation of much of the world. There was a failure to recognise that the objective moral high ground from which universal philosophical pronouncements were made was actually community-conditioned.

The contemporary thinkers who have pointed out the flimsiness of the philosophical emperor's garments have performed a public service. Where they, in turn, have got it seriously wrong is when they infer that because universal judgments are on shakier ground than previously supposed, it can be presumed that one thing is as "true" as any other. This simply isn't so. The stark judgment that Hitler was an evil bastard is entirely defensible.

Critical solidarity means, though, that as well as making these judgments, we in the west must attend carefully to the critique of others. For instance, the western country with the highest Christian churchgoing rate in the world executes people for crimes they committed as juveniles, and sends adults with mental deficiencies to the electric chair. That is barbarism by any standard.

A Muslim critique of Britain – if we could but open our ears and hear it – would challenge our grotesque enthronement of the individual adult, our unprotesting submission to the worst excesses of market-driven modernity, our piggishness in the midst of famine, the yobbishness and incivility which runs through all classes of our national life, the ghastly celebrity culture which turns the shallow Kilroys into national icons, our quickness to abort inconvenient foetuses, and our treatment of the problematic elderly. That's just for starters.

Are we capable of hearing – really hearing – such a critique? While we rightly condemn acts of barbarism and ask why the voices of Muslim protest against theocratic fascism seem so faint, can we get off our moral high horses and attend carefully to an eastern "take" on our collusion in the trade rules which disadvantage the underprivileged of the world? We would also be compelled to defend our nuclear arsenal in the Clyde while we threaten countries suspected of harbouring weapons of mass destruction.

All of this could make for a much more interesting pub hearing. Being a bar-room pundit – like being the editor of a tabloid newspaper – means never having to say you're sorry. Both the speaking and the hearing of unpalatable truths, in the context of a generous undergirding of universal exchange, can make human life a glorious rather than a mean business.

Critical solidarity. Rejoice in the diverse richness of other cultures. Speak out about injustices wherever they occur and whoever might be offended. Take on board the informed critiques of those who turn a searchlight on our way of life. Think of that poor girl dangling from the crane in the public square, and weep.

No island is an island

The windscreen wipers were going at double speed – welcome back to Scotland – as we headed up the A9 on Tuesday after two weeks in foreign parts. On reaching the blessed Scrabster, the thought crossed my mind that it would be nice to take a ten minute drive through a tunnel under the Pentland Firth and be sitting with a cup of tea in the electronic croft in no time at all.

These musings didn't go down too well with the electronic crofterina. We had been discussing *The Herald*'s report that Orkney Islands Council was investigating the possibility of an underground link between South Ronaldsay and John o' Groats. The Luddette lady is adamantly of the view that such a venture would spoil Orkney. She, the romantic soul, would prefer to lurch around on a bubbling sea for an hour and a half in the maintenance of some notion of island purity, an idea whose attractions somehow elude me.

To be fair, the whole business is more complex than I'm making it out to be. Digging a tunnel between Orkney and mainland Scotland is more than a matter of convenience and costs. Kindly allow the electronic crofter to guide you through an explosive issue which is about to create unpredictable waves.

Let's start by running back the film. Some weeks ago, Jeremy Baster, the council's director of development services, suggested that tunnels linking some of Orkney's smaller islands to the main island would be of economic benefit to the northern archipelago. This idea was received with great enthusiasm. Such a hub would encourage people to live on the smaller isles, and work on mainland Orkney. A bold move like this could keep wee island schools open.

The Council invited engineering expert Eivind Grov from Norway – which has 24 sub-sea links – to make a presentation. Once a new paradigm captures the mind, new possibilities suddenly open up. What about a tunnel between Orkney and mainland Scotland?

To understand the excitement generated by this proposition, it's essential to know that good, dependable transport is Orkney's holy grail. Not only does it encourage tourism, it makes possible the effective transportation of Orkney's high-pedigree livestock on which the island economy depends.

Hence the attraction of a tunnel. A short drive underneath the turbulent nine-mile stretch of water between Orkney and mainland Scotland would not only make the journey between the northern isles and the central belt considerably quicker, it would remove the unpredictability of the sea crossing.

Wind forward to this week. Eivind Grov apparently wowed the Council. A tunnel was, he said, a feasible option. Costs? Initial estimates, based on Norwegian models, would be in the region of £100m. You have to set against that the regular subsidies paid by the Scottish Executive to the ferry company NorthLink, and the £50m replacement costs for a new boat every 20 years.

So that's all right, then? Well, wait a minute. What was it they said in the beginning about the cost of the

Scottish parliament building? And there are other things which need to be factored in.

Greater accessibility means more tourists. What is the tipping point at which an increase in tourism actually destroys the tourist attraction? There are social issues as well. There is comparatively little crime in Orkney. Many people don't lock their house or their car. A tunnel would mean that some ruffians could come over in a van, clean up, and shoot offski through the wondrous tunnel. Far be it from me to suggest that thugs from the sooth could destroy Orkney's quality of life (*Don't bottle it, Ron, that's what you are suggesting. – Ed.*), but you can see that there are issues here.

Not only that, the electronic crofterina points out that beautiful islands are things that you sail to with dignity and reverence, not that you approach by crawling along some grubby hole in the ground. That's what islands are all about.

Ah, but no man is an island, entire of itself, said the 16th century poet John Donne. (*Get on with it, Ron. – Ed.*) Is an island with a tunnel to the mainland still an island? Friends, there are metaphysical issues here.

Well, what do I think? The electronic crofterina has nailed her colours firmly to Northlink's mast, and I am tempted to nail my colours firmly to the fence. However, columnists are supposed to have firm opinions about everything (as long as you don't ask us to be consistent).

On bad days, the Pentland Firth can be purgatorial. (*How can a man who voluntarily watches Cowdenbeath Football Club complain about 90 minutes of purgatory? – Ed.*) So I incline towards the tunnel. Not only that, your crofter could still pose as a wise, salt-encrusted wayfarer, while having a subterranean escape route. It's all a bit Freudian.

The crofterina doesn't like this. I think we're going to need a bridge across troubled waters. Never send to know for whom the bell tolls, said Donne, it tolls for thee. Talking of tolls....(*Enough. – Ed.*)

George eats up the Pope's porridge

T he body language says it all. The Emperor sits forward on his chair, clearly nervous and uncomfortable. Rather than appearing imperial, the most powerful man in the world looks like a schoolboy who has been called into the headmaster's study. His eyes are fixed upon the pontiff, who is wagging an index finger as he speaks words of rebuke. It is a transfixing image.

Pope John Paul II, says the Herald, delivered "a humiliating rebuke" to President George W. Bush over Iraq. The frail, 84-year-old pontiff left his guest in no doubt about his displeasure, saying, "Deplorable events have come to light which have troubled the civic and religious conscience of all."

It's worth freezing the picture right there, in order to look more closely at what is going on. First, though, we need some historical context. Let the story of a much more powerful papal rebuke set the scene.

It is the year 1074. The recently elected Pope Gregory VII has just banned, among other things, clerical marriage. It is not a move which goes down well in the Roman empire. The German clergy, touchingly, declare that they would rather give up their lives than their wives.

Emperor Henry IV accuses the pope of innovation, and alleges, correctly, that the pontiff is inciting the Saxons to take arms against the emperor. Henry calls on Gregory to come down from the throne of Saint Peter, which he has usurped by the sword.

The pope doesn't mess about. He declares Henry deposed as emperor. He also excommunicates him, which is virtually consigning him to hell. Quickly reading the political runes, Henry decides to make a penitential pilgrimage. With his wife and infant son in tow, he sets out across the Alps in freezing conditions. Henry goes to meet Pope Gregory at the castle of Canossa. Clad as a suppliant in white wool, the emperor stands barefoot in the snow, seeking admission. The pontiff keeps him waiting for three days. Henry agrees to strict conditions of obedience to the Church, and is readmitted to holy communion.

Now that is real power. It is also vanished power. As Stalin pointed out disparagingly, modern popes have no legions. So is there any connection between the story of Henry's apparent last hooray and George Goes to the Vatican? As the leader of the greatest superpower since the Roman empire, President Bush, though not clad in white wool, felt compelled to take the finger-wagging and eat up his porridge.

Why? It's the election, stupid.

Pope John Paul II does not have Gregory's power to depose emperors, but countervailing moral authority can influence democratic elections. George W. Bush cannot forget that he did not win the majority of American votes last time around, and that it was only the celestial intervention of St Chad of Florida that gained him the presidency. Roman Catholics make up 27 percent of the American electorate, and if the Protestant born-again Bush is to win again he needs a good chunk of the

Catholic vote. A few minutes of squirming in a Vatican chair is worth the price.

Switch to America. The Catholic presidential candidate, John Kerry, is in trouble with his church. While he is a regular attender at mass, he supports abortion under certain conditions, as well as civil unions for same sex couples. He also supports marriage for Roman Catholic priests. The Democratic candidate's own archbishop, Boston's Sean O'Malley, has said that Catholic politicians who do not conform to church doctrine should voluntarily stay away, adding that they "shouldn't dare come to communion".

There is an irony here. When John F. Kennedy sought to become the first Catholic to win the White House in 1960, he had to overcome accusations from non-Catholics that he would follow the bidding of the pope. Now, Mr. Kerry faces accusations from within his own church that he is not following the pope's bidding closely enough.

The issue is causing furious debate within the Catholic Church in America. Senator Kerry stands with his church on many social justice issues, including immigration, poverty, health care and the death penalty. It is abortion which is the sticking point. But why stop there? Why not withdraw communion from any Catholic candidate who, like many Catholics throughout the world, does not follow the Vatican teaching on artificial birth control?

The churches have a legitimate role to play in a democratic society. It's good to see President Bush get a moral grilling on Iraq from someone of the spiritual stature of John Paul II. It's also right that Senator Kerry should be questioned by his own faith community about issues that really matter. But to use holy communion as a political tool is to turn the sublime into what is worse than ridiculous.

No wonder George Bush, who is much closer to the Pope on personal moral issues than John Kerry, gulped down his medicine. He may even remember the historical postscript: the restored pseudo-groveller, Henry IV, got his own back by imprisoning Pope Gregory and setting up another pope who crowned him emperor once again.

Visceral feelings about life after death

When you pass away, pop your clogs, hand in your chips, fall off the perch – or whatever your euphemism of choice is – is that the end of the matter? When your earthly remains are laid in the earth or shoved into the furnace, is that the termination of your personal story – or is there another thrilling instalment to come?

Anyone searching the television schedules for a semi-sensible religious programme over the Easter weekend would have done so in vain. Fortunately, stuck in the small print of BBC Radio Scotland's listings was a real gem. Called Life After Death: This is My Story, the programme consisted largely of interviews with people about how they understood the end of their mortal existence.

The action began with a conversation between an elderly couple and the programme's presenter, Mark Stephen. The couple said that after death they were sure that, as believers in Jesus Christ, they would go to heaven to be with the Lord. Mark confessed that he was not a believer, so what would happen to him? They didn't shirk it. Unless he changed his mind, he would go to hell.

What made the interview riveting was that the elderly couple were Mark Stephen's parents.

They sounded kindly and decent people. They clearly loved their son, and he loved them, but that was the way life was. As a non-believer, he was destined for the fiery furnaces.

It was a stunning piece of radio. The normality, the casualness even, made this heart-stopping moment all the more grotesque. Two good people were telling their son that he was destined for eternal destruction *because he failed to believe certain propositions*. His inability to believe that a Jewish teacher who walked in Palestine 2000 years ago was the Son of God – Stephen made it clear that much as he wanted to believe he couldn't – apparently condemned him to an afterlife of punishment. We'll return to this point later.

Over many centuries, large numbers of human beings have believed that when they die, their life will continue in some form. There is something in the human condition which rebels against the notion that this life is all there is. In my days as a minister, before returning to the less than gospel-greedy fleshpots of hackdom, I often felt that same visceral stab when I stood at bleak gravesides.

After every funeral, I would go back to the house and share a dram with the mourners. In the relaxation following the tension of the day, many a person would say to me, "I'm an atheist myself, but let me tell you about this religious experience I once had....."

But we live in a scientific age, and for many people of integrity, religious belief is not possible. The notion of a "soul" – an intangible something at the core of my being which makes me who I am – is in decline, in Europe at least. Neuroscience claims even to find places in the brain which are responsible for religious experiences.

Religious people are vulnerable to the accusation that their faith is wishful thinking, masking a deep need for security. This Freudian sword is double-edged, though. Might the atheist be unconsciously bodyswerving the unpalatable notion of ultimate judgment? Discuss.

Some telegrammatic observations: Consciousness itself is a profound mystery. Science is now much less reductionistic and more open than it used to be. Researchers investigating 'near-death' experiences say they have found evidence to suggest that consciousness can continue to exist after the brain has ceased to function. Neither the existence of God nor an afterlife can be proved.

Here's how I would answer Mark Stephen's questions. Do I believe in God? Yes, but I know less about the sacred now than I thought I did when I was 20. Do I believe in life after death? Yes, though what it might be like I haven't a scooby. It's beyond human imagination and language. What about eternity? Can't get my mind around the word.

Any images we might or might not have about an afterlife will depend on our image of God. Personally, I can't worship a God who slaughters millions of people because they don't *believe* certain things – Slobodan Milosevic is rightly on trial for much less than that. Nor do I want to spend eternity flattering and brown-nosing some ghastly genocidal tyrant. I'm putting my theological money on Jesus not being a misleading icon of the divine, though I recognize that that particular imagery has a lot to do with the tradition and the community in which I was brought up.

And I do, at the side of these open graves, still want to affirm – often in the teeth of the available evidence – that love is not defeated by death. Irrational? Maybe.

Unscientific? Possibly. But faith is more like a love affair with God than it is about a tick-list of beliefs. And there are nailprints of suffering love in the hands that – I hope – will one day wipe away all tears.

I'll rat on caring Kerry

So we've had Kerry the resolute, Kerry the Vietnam veteran, Kerry the caring, and now, to top it all, Kerry the hamster lover. As the Democrats seek to re-invent the rather aloof John Kerry as a warm-hearted presidential candidate, they wheel out Alexandra, the candidate's 30-year-old daughter, to tell the touching story of Licorice the hamster. It is currently gripping the nation.

Alexandra told how the heroic John Kerry once dived off a dock to save her hamster from a "watery doom". What's more, the Vietnam hero then administered heart massage to the ailing rodent. Yes, heart massage.

If this doesn't swing the election away from George W Bush, then I don't know what will. A president who gives heart massage to a hamster, after diving from a rock to save it. Beat that! Not even St Francis of Assisi administered mouth-to-mouth resuscitation to a barely-breathing rodent.

I must confess I'm being more than a little disingenuous here. It so happens that I know more about this story than I've given away so far. Because I was there. Well, not quite; I was nearly there. Let me explain.

After the dramatic rescue, Licorice was in intensive care. An alert went out for a healer with special empathy for rodents. It just so happened that my now world famous book, Donald Dewar Ate My Hamster, exploded on to the New York best-seller lists at the same time as pale little Licorice lay a-dying. It was surely divine providence that my moving tale of how I had rescued a hamster from the jaws of Scotand's famously ravenous first minister hit America just as Licorice was having a mirror held up to his sweet little mouth.

I responded to the call with compassion, alacrity and my press officer. The direct flight by Concorde from Kirkwall was over in moments. I stepped down the stairway with the kind of double-breasted power walk which is now mimicked by George W Bush and Tony Blair. I was completely in charge. The Cadillac sped me to the private hospital, where I authoritatively resisted Teresa Heinz Kerry's kisses and strode into the sickness room, brushing past John Kerry, who was wearing a Superman suit. I'm like that when I'm on a mission. No-one dare cross my path when I'm focused on a dying hamster.

Little Licorice was wired up to ten machines in the darkened room. I ordered that the apparatus be removed forthwith. Teresa Heinz Kerry simpered. She knew she was in the presence of a masterful man. Then I cleared the room. Striding over to Licorice, I looked into his eyes, indeed deep into his soul.

"Licorice," I commanded, "Get up at once! You're malingering. You're enjoying all this attention, and this expensive care. I've met your kind before. You're nothing but a bed-blocker."

Licorice's eyes locked on to mine, then a smile crossed his little face. "My hero," he said. Just like that.

A talking hamster. Is there no end to God's providence? I clicked on my tape recorder.

"Tell me what really happened," I said.

"Only if you give me one of these Krispy Kremes," he replied sweetly, pointing to a plateful of doughnuts. I co-operated.

"Don't believe that crap about John Kerry diving in from a rock," said Licorice. "I was never in any danger, in fact I was swimming in shallow water. Then Mr Kerry waded in, up to his ankles, and picked me up. I didn't need rescuing at all."

"What happened next?" I asked.

"Another Krispy Kreme," he replied. I stretched out my hand.

"Alexandra was crying hysterically – she's an actress, remember, and she was screaming for an ambulance. I immediately feigned death. The only time I was actually in danger was when Mr Kerry started beating my chest and giving me mouth-to-mouth. It was terrible.

"I decided to milk it for all I could get, since that's what Mr Kerry was doing. I knew that some day I'd be paraded at the Democratic convention, with tears running down everybody's cheeks. I'd be feted with Krispy Kremes. Which reminds me...."

I obliged. I clicked off my tape recorder, and called in the family and the medics. They were astounded to see Licorice sitting up in bed, eating a doughnut. Alexandra cried dramatically. The weeping Teresa hugged me passionately. Big John Kerry smiled modestly as the cameras flashed. I slipped out into the dark night, and hailed a taxi to the airport. Within what seemed like minutes, I was back at the electronic croft.

It could have been worse, I thought. It could have been Tony Blair who had rescued the bloody hamster.

He would have been on television, bottom lip quivering, calling Licorice "the people's hamster". I couldn't have coped with that.

In the meantime, I still have that explosive tape recording. It has the power to alter the course of history. By the beginning of November, as John Kerry is head-to-head with Dubya, the electronic crofter is going to be very, very rich. My dear friend Teresa will pay the asking price.

Noah makes apocalyptic comeback

The wee man who used to shuffle through the crowd declaring that the end of the world is nigh now has a suit, several academic degrees, and – thanks to 21st century communications – a world-wide audience. The European Space Agency's chief scientist, Dr Bernard Foing, yesterday advocated the establishment of a DNA library on the moon.

Dr Foing, who is head of Europe's moon missions, is concerned that if the earth were destroyed, there would be little or nothing left of the rich diversity of life on the planet. Hence his suggestion that there should be a repository for the DNA of every single species of animal and plant on the moon.

" If there were a catastrophic collision on earth or a nuclear war, you could place some samples of earth's biosphere, including humans, on the moon," he said, adding that the earth could be repopulated afterwards – though precisely what " afterwards" might be like is a good question.

Search through the memory traces, and you may recall a similar plan. Yes, you've got it. Noah's Ark. If you think that Dr Foing might be going over the top, remember – they laughed at Noah. When he was frantically nailing together cubits and cubits of cedar wood in his back garden while the sun split the skies, he must have been the neighbourhood joke. Then, when the rain started to come down like a Glasgow Fair holiday, with the animals safely packed inside, doubt must have spread around the bungalows. By the time the torrents had reached their peak, Noah was waving while the neighbours were drowning, and the floating repository of DNA samples of every creature on earth enjoyed the 40-day cruise.

Many ancient civilizations have a flood myth. It's as if there were a corporate memory of an earth-shaking catastrophe which was both an endtime and a beginning time. It's an archetypal story about a god who is fed up with the way his human experiment is going, and determines to make a new start.

Is Dr Bernard Foing the new 21st century Noah? Does he know something that we don't know? Does he have a secret word from the Lord? That's not how he puts it. He is a scientist who is reading the runes – or maybe even looking for funding. Europe's first probe to the moon is due in November, the first of what Dr Foing hopes will be a fleet of robotic spacecraft. This makes possible the building of a lunar colony, complete with its own DNA library.

It's not surprising that biblical imagery should make a comeback in apocalyptic times. The sight of the twin towers of the World Trade Center pouring down like molten lava into the living rooms of the world recalled the fate of the pretentious tower of Babel. There is a difference, though. In Noah's day, only the deity could destroy the earth. Today, that awesome power is in human hands. After the 20th century slaughter of nearly 100 million people, the new century's chilling technology of mass death is accompanied by the impatient pawing of four horses in the apocalyptic stables.

We live in strange times. This country of ours has vast wealth. Advances in health services have extended our expectation of life dramatically. We are no longer prey to pestilence. We travel abroad like medieval princes. And yet, we are inwardly bracing ourselves against an unnamed catastrophe, like Berti Vogts on a normal day at the office. Survey after survey reveals an underlying pessimism, which runs into fatalism.

When barbarism is combined with high-tech skills and a willingness to die for a cause – and the devastating consequences are transmitted live across the globe – a fearful insecurity is let loose in the world. The dangers are real, but the biggest one is that of our own crippling sense of impotence. If we feel we are merely bit players in a deterministic cosmic drama, we surrender responsibility for the fate of the earth. Then the human die truly is cast.

Fearful cowering and fatalism diminish us. The task before us now, if we would not perish, said Teilhard de Chardin, is to shake off our ancient prejudices and rebuild the earth. In the best of theology, God and humans are co-creators. If the sins of the fathers are not to be visited on future generations, justice – and human connectedness – have to be at the heart of our world. Rather than more technological "fixes", we need a less fearful and more generous posture.

The image of a DNA library on the moon is one to haunt our dreams. The ancient endtime story narrates that when Noah and the ark returned after the floods subsided, the deity put a rainbow in the sky as a sign that he wouldn't run that particular horror movie again. For many people in the west, that god has died. My own, minority, take on it is that he has been taken hostage by fundamentalists. Isn't it time to set him – and ourselves – free?

109

Food for thought, if not for supper

"I have no name:
I am but two days old."
What shall I call thee?
"I happy am
Joy is my name."
Sweet joy befall thee!
   – William Blake, Songs of Innocence.

I f it were discovered that foetal tissue were a delicacy, would you eat it? That may be just about the most tasteless opening sentence to a newspaper column that you've ever read, but it goes right to the heart of the debate about abortion, and foetal experiment.

Its framing is not mine. The question was asked by Stanley Hauerwas, Professor of Theological Ethics at Duke University, when he was debating with a medical researcher. As I discovered when I met him at Duke a few months ago, this hard-swearing Methodist son of a Texas bricklayer – who enrages conservatives and liberals alike, and who was recently named by Time magazine as the most brilliant theologian in America – believes that when we discuss ethical issues, we need to know what we are talking about.

110

So does film maker Julia Black. Her disturbing *My Foetus*, screened on Channel 4, provided food for thought, if not for supper.

"One in three women in Britain will have an abortion," said Julia, "but we continue to shy away from the reality of the procedure. It is easy to be pro-choice without challenging yourself about what that means. I needed to be convinced that abortion is a morally legitimate procedure even after knowing what it involves, and I wanted to take viewers on the same journey."

It was quite a journey. The graphic images of aborted foetuses did not make for easy viewing. The 23-week-old foetus, sucking its thumb in the womb, was, well, like a baby. Simply to favour abortion as "pro-choice" is to diminish what's at stake – the killing of a helpless potential human being.

Julia Black made the film while she was pregnant with her second child. Her first pregnancy, 14 years ago, ended in abortion, and now she wanted to ask: "What was it I killed?". Is a foetus in any way human? (Hence the crude question at the beginning of this piece.)

By breaking the taboo against showing an actual abortion, Black provided a public service in what was a sensitive, if gruelling, piece of television. Ever since the programme was announced there has been furious controversy, with some liberals calling for it to be banned. Liberals, of course, don't have anything as crude as dogmas: they only have blessed assumptions which are so full of obvious commonsense and right thinking that they don't even need to be justified.

It is deeply ironic that television shows sex, violence and bloody warfare all the time, yet baulks at a realistic showing of what actually happens when an abortion is carried out. My Foetus was shunted till after 11 pm to avoid frightening the lieges.

111

Lying behind the abortion debate is a huge mountain of human misery and desperation. All the evidence shows that women have abortions for two basic reasons: fear that they cannot handle the financial and physical demands of the child, and fear that having the child will destroy relationships that are important to them.

Still further back lies a whole series of troubling questions about sexual pressure, economic assumptions, cultural expectations, and financial support for young mothers. Many factors combine to make the thought of another child intolerable. The enthronement of individual adult choice above all other rights skews the debate. When abortion is used as a form of contraception, or where it is presented as a life-style choice, we are truly in perverse territory.

The position of the Roman Catholic Church is straightforward. The foetus has an absolute right to life, and to destroy it is murder. This stance, which is largely based around the commandment, "thou shalt not kill", has the virtue of clarity and consistency. The problems come with particular circumstances, such as the gang-rape of a 10-year-old girl by HIV-infected men. And where the mother's life is endangered, whose rights shall prevail? Should a 20-year-old mother with two young children be allowed to die? What is the compassionate decision which needs to be made here?

The commandment not to kill is relativised by giving a clean bill of moral health to soldiers, or by allowing an unborn child to die as a result of medication to the mother (ie not by actively terminating the pregnancy), yet is absolutised in the case of abortion. It seems to me that complete consistency can only be maintained by casuistry. I also think that for those who find abortion morally repugnant under any circumstances, a responsible family planning programme has to be on the agenda.

Abortion should surely be an absolute last-resort choice rather than a first-line response. A society which regards abortion as simply a privatized area of moral decision-making has lamentably failed in its obligation to protect the vulnerable. Julia Black's *Foetus* has thankfully brought new realism into what ought to be a compassionate public conversation.

The Son of Cod on eBay

What a wondrous world we live in! A woman who found an image of the Virgin Mary in her cheese toastie is £14,000 the richer, after selling the sacred object on the internet auction site eBay. Not only that, Diana Duyser and her 10-year-old toasted cheese sandwich are set to visit the UK as part of a world tour. Yes, a world tour for a cheese sandwich.

The holy toastie was bought by an online casino whose executives said they were willing to spend "as much as it took" to own the sandwich. Steve Baker, chief executive of the Canada-based GoldenPalace.com, said breathlessly: "We knew right away we had to have it. We think our customers around the world will really get a kick out of seeing the sandwich at the Taj Mahal, at Red Square, at the Eiffel Tower."

I'm sure he's right. The Taj Mahal will fade into insignificance beside a cheese toastie. Asked if there were plans to bring the relic to Scotland, Mr Baker said: "Sure. We want the whole world to share in this miracle."

Quite right, too. I would hate to think that Scotland might be excluded from viewing a 10-year-old toastie. This column believes that the sacred object should be borne aloft down the Royal Mile, followed by Martin O'Neill with his arm around a vulnerable Queen, and a procession of Scottish entrepreneurs, COSLA representatives, lunatics and senior clerics. The toastie should then be laid before an awed Holyrood, while Cardinal O'Brien and the Moderator lead a grateful nation in prayer. Donald Dewar, thou shouldst be living at this hour! He would have simply scoffed the holy sandwich.

Ten years ago, Mrs Duyser, from Hollywood, Florida, was so certain it was the image of the Virgin on the toastie that she kept it in a plastic box above her bed to watch over her. Yes, dear friends, she's been watched over by a cheese sandwich in a Tupperware box all that time. I find that deeply moving. Thankfully, she unselfishly decided to share the toastie with the world. In modern terms, that means flogging it on eBay. There were 100,000 hits on the site when she put her Virgin Mary apparition up for sale. Who says that religion is dying?

There's more. The face of Jesus has appeared on a fishcake in Canada. It's worth reading that glorious sentence again. Fred Whaun, from Ontario, burned the fishcake last year while he was making his dinner. It was his son who first spotted the likeness to Jesus Christ on the charred object. It's not every day that you see the Son of Cod. Now Fred has decided to share his fishcake with the world. Yes, it's on eBay.

There is a peedie problem here, mind you. Nobody has a clue what the Virgin Mary or Jesus of Nazareth looked like. None. The familiar images of a pale Mary clad in Italian robes are fantasies. The flesh-and-blood Mary would have been a dark-skinned 11- or 12-year-old Jewish peasant girl. So Our Lady of the Cheese Toastie might have born a passing resemblance to a Renaissance painting of the Virgin, but that's about it. And the Fishcake Messiah probably looked like Robert Redford with 60 degree burns.

As institutional religion collapses, credulity rises. The study of Aquinas has given way to the raptured gazing upon a mouldy toastie. Jesus said if you really want to see his face, feed the poor and visit the prisoners – not quite the same as peering at a fishcake or even a bleeding statue. And when credulity meets venality, eBay, the great auction-room in the sky, is the perfect vehicle. Postmodern online shopping nirvana is only a mouse-click away.

Let me remind you of the Christmas story. When the Emperor Dubya heard of the birth of yet another swarthy trouble-maker, he calleth his Three Wise Persons, Rummi, Condi and Toni (with his blind guide, David) unto him. And he saith unto them: 'Go follow the star on your GPS monitor and find the baby.' And when they draweth nigh unto the byre, they presenteth to the child gold, frankincense and myrrh. Then they texteth directions to the house of whiteness from their satellite phones.

The Emperor's flashing neon sign in the sky, saying 'Mission Accomplished', alarmed the shepherds in the fields, but while Dubya loadeth his thermonuclear Christmas present for Bethlehem, the holy asylum seekers snucketh down to Egypt. Then Joseph, the boy's father – though he failed a DNA paternity test – looketh again at the gold, frankincense and myrrh, and saith unto himself: 'I could get serious shekels for this little lot, I mean I would like to share these with the world, and it came to pass that he put them on eBay, and there were a million Hittites on the website. The eventual winner was Osama, a multi-millionaire, of 1 Main Street, Karachi, who turned out to be a former business associate of Rummi. And the angels saith, 'Be afraid, be very afraid.'

116

Beckhams in the crib? Pass me the blue nun

I f you're going to send out a Christmas card
to the world, nothing can trump having an actual
photograph of Jesus Christ himself on the front.
Well, it has come to pass, as they say in the Bible. The
messiah stands there, with a worshipping angel at his
side, in a pose which is both studied and casual. O, come
let us adore him! Yes, Tony sends you his best wishes for
the Christmas season.

The photograph of the prime minister and his lady
wife, on the front of Tuesday's Herald, was
two-fingers-down-the-throat material. It was the stuff
which makes luvvy image-makers coo and normal
sentient beings throw up. Our irritating peedie messiah
with the wrinkles smoothed out was dressed in trendy
gear to make him look youthful. It looked like a
grotesque photo-shoot for a Next catalogue.

Don't you know it's Christmas, Tone? Christmas
isn't actually about you at all. It's the season of peace
and goodwill. Isn't there something missing from your
Christmas card? Okay, I get your cheesy drift: whatever
you do, don't talk about the war. The bodies stacked up
behind that Gothic-style arch at Chequers are not, repeat
not, to be photographed. In the name of Christ, nothing
must be done to spoil the Tone-fest. Anyone pointing out

117

that the emperor's casual clothes are blood-spattered will be taken away by the Home Secretary and given an unfair trial.

Where is sanity to be found this Christmas? Don't bother to head for Madame Toussaud's, to view their nativity scene. It features, I kid you not, David Beckham as Joseph and Posh Spice as Mary: yet another adoring lady beside a self-obsessed man. Christmas can do your head in.

Last week, in my piece about the image of the Virgin Mary on a 10-year-old cheese toastie and the face of Jesus on a fishcake, I did a mild satire on the Christmas story, featuring Rummi, Condi and Toni as the Three Wise Persons. This week I feel like the American columnist who said that he gave up writing satire when Henry Kissinger was awarded the Nobel peace prize. Madame Tussaud, God bless her, has Tony Blair, President Bush and the Duke of Edinburgh as the three wise men. Just as well there were no actual Palestinians present, or the Chookie Embra might have caused a little frisson by wondering aloud who all the darkies were. That's the price you pay when you involve real-life celebrities.

The three shepherds who complete the scene are the bible-quoting gangster from Pulp Fiction, Samuel L Jackson; Hugh Grant, complete with a lamb in hand; and comedian Graham Norton. A sultry angel, none other than Kylie Minogue, strikes a seductive pose above the manger. Honestly, I'm not making this up.

The celebrity nativity scene was created after 300 visitors were asked which celebrities they would like to see in which roles. They voted overwhelmingly for the Beckhams in the central roles. The people have spoken. Pass me the Blue Nun. The world is steadily going off its corporate heid.

The utterly unspeakable celebrity culture has taken over everything else, so why not the nativity? In Italy, there is nothing new in contemporary figures featuring in the nativity scene, but they are always onlookers. With a weary sigh, I acknowledge that it was only a matter of time before the celebrities gatecrashed the main event. Newsflash: the holy couple in the crib scene are currently building a £120,000 play castle as a Christmas present for their sons Brooklyn and Romeo. That means they are just the people to represent a pair of poor asylum seekers who had to flee for their lives. O Little Town of Becklehem! No, it's impossible to parody a parody.

We should be thankful for small mercies, though. We were spared the sight of Janet Street-Porter as the Virgin Mary. Or John Prescott as a donkey. Or Jackie Bird as Mrs Herod. Or Prince Charles as a tree. The real Joseph would have said: "I'm not a celebrity, get me out of here".

The best antidote to all this is a viewing of the hilarious Monty Python "Life of Brian". It should be shown on the telly every Christmas. The film opens with three wise men on camels, arriving at a tumbledown house. They go in, put down their expensive gifts and prostrate themselves before a new-born child, much to the bafflement of the bairn's watching single mother. Minutes later, they come back angrily and snatch the gifts away again. Wrong hoose.

The irony of all this nativity business is that the original Mary and Joseph were the opposite of celebrities. And Jesus wasn't born in Beckingham Palace, but in cowshed. In his short life, he spoke up for the poor and the dispossessed.

Which reminds me: according to yesterday's report, the gap between the rich and the poor in Britain has grown under New Labour. And the poor of our cities can expect to live seven years less than their middle-class neighbours over the wall. And a Merry Christmas from Tony.

Dying to get on the telly

S ome people will do anything to get on to the telly. They're dying to do it, literally. The corpses which are dissected nightly this week on Channel 4's "Anatomy for Beginners" gave their permission, in the days when they were in breathing mode, to be cut up in public.

Mine host with the magic scissors is the controversial anatomist Dr Gunther von Hagens. The German is felt by some to be a vulgar showman, and I expected to be somewhat repelled by the programme. Instead, I have been riveted by it. The dear man's passion is to democratize anatomy and to allow the punters to see its wonders for themselves. The commentaries by John Lee, Professor of Pathology at the Hull York Medical School, add a reassuring note of, well, British gravitas.

The respectful filleting of the corpses is not for the squeamish, but it makes for compulsive viewing. These are very material, flesh and blood, demonstrations of the vulnerability of the physical; they also provide evidence of the sheer awesomeness of the human. Dr von Hagens carefully removed the brain and the spinal cord of one cadaver to reveal an internal communications system of such sublime sophistication that it makes our most cutting-edge computers seem like primitive toys.

What is a human being? For starters, it's a creature whose heart routinely pumps 6,300 gallons of blood through 96,000 miles of blood vessels every day. And did you known, dear reader, that the DNA from all the genes of your 75 trillion body cells would fit into a box the size of an ice cube – but if all this DNA were unwound and joined together, the string would stretch from the earth to the sun and back more than 400 times? Now I don't carry around all this information in my 25 billion sparkling brain cells, but I know that it's utterly amazing. What beautiful, awkward, appalling, puzzling, creatures we are.

Another TV programme which raises much more troubling questions about the nature of the human is BBC2's Auschwitz: the Nazis and the Final Solution. The series follows the trail of evil from the origins of Auschwitz as a place to hold Polish political prisoners, through the Nazi solution for what they called "the Jewish problem" to the development of the camp as a mechanised factory for mass murder.

What is most chilling about this brilliant series is the way in which apparently rational people calmly discuss the mass extermination of fellow human beings as if they are talking about a local public transport problem. They coolly arrange for revved-up motor bikes to drown out the haunting screams of the dying. Everything is carefully minuted, giving each death-dealing meeting the feel of a community council in uniforms. Then camp commandant Rudolf Hoess goes off home to play with his children and listen to Beethoven on the gramophone.

The Nazis had an answer to the question about the value of Jews, gypsies and gays. The victims' rings were taken off to be sold, and gold fillings were removed from their teeth. Their skin was used to make officers' lampshades and their hair was taken off for cushions. Each human being might be worth a couple of pounds.

What does it mean to be human? Dr von Hagens, for all his showmanship, is echoing the word of the ancient psalmist that we are "fearfully and wonderfully made". Another Hebrew poet cries that human beings are created a little lower than the angels. One of the several writers of the book of Genesis insists that humans are made in the image of God. I pitch my tent – in the teeth of a grotesque tsunami – with those who want to insist that the stamp of the divine is hidden within each of us.

When we lose the transcendent rooting of our frail humanity, when the intrinsic worth of each human being loses its ontological moorings and slips into a bottomless utilitarian marsh, humanity is in profoundly disturbing trouble. The Nazi Euthanasia Committee, which provided its own final solution to the "problem" of the mentally and physically disabled, signals the route of the runaway moral train, freighted with psalm-singing children in mortal terror, as it heads remorselessly towards the buffers.

We humans are touched with bright wings, made for glory. At our best, we are creatures capable of supreme loving sacrifices. We are also capable of doing things that no other animal would do. James Froude said, "Man is the only animal to whom the torture and death of his fellow creatures is amusing in itself."

In one concentration camp, the Jewish inmates decided to put God on trial. The deity was found guilty as charged. The meeting broke up when someone pointed out that it was time for evening prayers. On this Holocaust Memorial day, I want to side with those who are determined to put humanity and God in the dock and to demand answers to charges of committing crimes against humanity; and also to cry a broken and a wounded Hallelujah.

Why I don't want to be called a Christian

The angel spake unto the virgin Kimberley and saith unto her, 'The spirit shall come upon thee and thou shalt bear a son, and he shall be called, er, the son of David, or the son of Simon, or even the son of Stephen, and the boy shalt have a fast-tracked nanny. The virgin Kimberley pondereth these things in her tabloids, and accuseth David, servant of the Emperor Blairod. And Blairod saith with an quivering lip, "I am absolutely certain that my servant David is innocent. He is a splendid Home Wrecketary; in fact he is the People's Home Wrecketary. Not only that, he locketh up people without trial. And we know where you liveth."

No, it doesn't quite work as a nativity narrative, does it? But it's not a million miles away from the question at the heart of this column two days before Christmas: is Britain a Christian country? Remember that Blairod and his servant David are both Christians. David may suffer from a memory deficit about troublesome paperwork and Antonius may easily become detached from inconvenient facts, but, what does that matter when you act "in good faith"?

So is Britain a Christian country? The question has been posed by David Hope, Archbishop of York, who

124

blamed "secularist tendencies" for what he saw as the country's abandonment of Christianity. Wait a minute, though. It all depends on what you mean.

Let me sharpen and personalise this: I don't really want to carry the "Christian" label any more – not because of lack of faith, but because the word itself carries too much ideological baggage. "Are you a Christian?" has become such a loaded question that I no longer care to answer it in the affirmative.

Why? Christianity has become an ugly credo. In its grossest and most commonly understood manifestations, it has been transformed into an all-singing, all-dancing, conquering ideology, backed up by a vastly expensive "shock and awe" military arsenal and supported by a god who acts like a psychopathic killer. As I write, I have on my study wall the searing words of the late, lamented, Professor Robert Carroll of Glasgow University: "Everywhere we look, ideology slouches along the freeways and autoroutes, sometimes carrying a cross, sometimes a sickle, sometimes a crescent, but always busy doing somebody in somewhere, somehow."

Led by an aggressive American theology of righteous empire and backed by fast-growing British expressions of religion which emphasise certainty and cannot tolerate ambiguity, the dominant Christian ideology is increasingly characterised by a hardline personal morality accompanied by an apocalyptic madness which undermines human rights in the so-called holy land. If this is what the "Christian" train is to be, I want to get off at the next station.

I watch with dismay as the white-hatted Christian cowboy in the White House throws his weight around the world. I watch with incredulity as my stage-struck, heavily made up, populist, authoritarian Christian prime minister shamelessly changes his reasons for going to war, and smilingly presides over a regime which incarcerates suspects indefinitely without trial and erodes civil rights for which people shed their blood. George Orwell, where are you now that we need you?

The most striking fact about all this Christian stuff is that it is utterly disconnected from the life and teachings of Jesus of Nazareth. The heart of the matter has been ripped out of the Christian body. The child of Bethlehem grew up to be a divine disturber of the peace. He identified with the poor, the dispossessed, the vulnerable, the outsider: and compounded that offence by saying that the divine power at the heart of the universe was like that. His radical message discomfited the powerful. He was banged up without proper trial and executed as an enemy of church and state. The dominant empire theology is no nearer to Bethlehem than the current crass consumer-fest.

In all the Christmas messages to reach the electronic croft, I was particularly touched by a Franciscan blessing: "May God bless you with discomfort at easy answers, half truths, and superficial relationships, so that you may live deep within your heart. May God bless you with anger at injustice, oppression, and exploitation of people, so that you may work for justice, freedom and peace. May God bless you with tears to shed for those who suffer from pain, rejection, starvation and war, so that you may reach out your hand to comfort them and to turn their pain to joy. May God bless you with enough foolishness to believe that you can make a difference in this world, so that you can do what others claim cannot be done."

It was sent to me by a Christian same-sex couple who have been together for more than 30 years, and whose commitment puts me to shame. Of course, in the year of Our Lord 2004, they have to live without a church blessing, while those who bless nuclear warheads in the name of the prince of peace have seats at the high table. "Christianity"? Thanks, but no thanks.

Into the jungle with Irn Broon

ordon in Africa: sounds like a film title. The pictures of the white-shirted Chancellor, sweating beside poor children and sitting with an AIDS victim, were quite touching in their awkwardness. The dour man from Fife made his determined way through the geographical and political terrain like David Livingstone; though instead of bearers he had a team of snappers. Was it merely yet another phase in the Downing Street wars, as some unkind cynics have suggested?

One thing for sure is that Irn Broon wouldn't have gone into the jungle with Tony Blair as his spear carrier, especially if Tone, sincere as ever, insisted on walking behind him. Let me say what I mean with a little story.

Two men were in the jungle one day when they heard the roar of a lion. The bigger of the two men immediately started to work out a strategy. His companion quickly whipped off his knapsack and pulled out a pair of trainers.

"What's the point of doing that?" asked the big man. "You can't run faster than a lion!"

"I don't need to" replied his already disappearing friend. "I only need to run faster than you."

128

The lumbering, heavy-jowled Gordon, like the Pope, wears the Doc Martens; fleet-of-foot Tony is the man with the flashy designer trainers in a race in which the spoils go to the swift and the nimble. The big man is the director of the big picture; his heavily made-up companion is the leading actor who holds the uncanny belief that he is every one of the characters he plays.

So was the African adventure all for show? With such a complex man as Gordon Brown there can be no simple answer to this or any other question, but to make a stab at it we need to journey backwards in time to a manse in Kirkcaldy.

The biggest acknowledged influence in the socialist Chancellor's life is not Karl Marx but the Rev Dr John Brown. A fine preacher, Gordon's father articulated a brand of Christianity which had a passion for social justice at its heart. Brown has already talked about the missionaries from Africa who came to the manse when he was a young man. In the 1950s and 1960s, the Kirk had some outstanding people in Africa, and their reports were highly influential in the break-up of the British government-supported undemocratic Central African Federation.

Gordon Brown's interest in Africa dates from these passionate debates. His concern for the Third World and the plight of Africa is no fad, but a longstanding and deep commitment. His fact-finding visit to Africa cannot be understood apart from this enduring commitment.

Brown's leadership on Third World debt relief has been outstanding over several years. His determination to put the matter of world poverty at the top of the agenda of this year's G8 summit at Gleneagles is entirely in character. In these last few days he has berated the world's wealthiest nations for missing their own poverty targets, said that he wanted the developing world and the West to "open their books" to public scrutiny, called for new international rules to stamp out corruption, advocated changes to trade rules which disadvantage poor countries, and persuaded Nelson Mandela to attend the G8 summit.

Amidst all the complexity which bears the name Gordon Brown, there is a genuine idealist. As a Presbyterian pragmatist, he is well enough acquainted with the doctrine of original sin to know that people won't go into the privacy of a British polling booth and simply vote for aid to Africa unless they feel themselves to be prosperous and secure. But he's also a big enough believer in the equally valid doctrine of original goodness to know that, as the overwhelming response to the Asian tsunami has shown, there is an innate human capacity for generosity.

What is most striking post-tsunami is that the "make poverty history" campaign has never had a better chance of making a breakthrough. There is more than one kind of climate change, and Gordon Brown has been a significant player in its creation.

Will the undoubtedly ambitious Brown ever be premier, or will he himself be history? He has already been described as "psychologically flawed" – how could one ever say that of a Fifer? – by no less a personage than Alistair Campbell. Takes one to know one. The knives are certainly out for this big beast in the political jungle.

I would like to see him get the top job – and not just because he would be the first member of the House of Commons Cowdenbeath Supporters Club to hold the office. For all his brooding sins and political plotting, Brown has a strategic, though non-utopian, vision for changing a world in which millions of children die in poverty each year. My fear, though, is that he will be devoured by a prowling lion while the smiling, impossible-to-shame spear carrier runs away with all the prizes.

Mercilous waves bring hard questions

A tidal wave which began in the Indian Ocean has poured into our living rooms and deposited stinking corpses all over our homes. Our domestic festive peace has been invaded. At a stroke, the taste for tales about the Beckham christenings in a specially constructed £100,000 chapel and the £1m diamond ring for Posh Spice turns to ashes in the mouth. The total-immersion baptism of death for more than 100,000 human beings raises more questions than we can handle in this season of goodwill.

It is hard for us to get a grip on the scale of this tragedy, so much so that it seems we can only handle the situation when the story has a kilt on it. "Scots tourists flee wave of death". As the early corpse count came in, it struck me that the equivalent of the population of Orkney – men, women and children – had been swept away. Then the figures doubled and doubled again, and will rise and rise.

The floodwaters bringing human detritus to our waking and sleeping consciousness has the capacity to undermine the carefully constructed foundations of our lives. The relentless, merciless waves bring questions about power and control, about vulnerability and planning, about human and even divine agency.

132

First, let me digress. It wasn't till I changed from being a city to an island dweller that I fully took on board the power of the elements. Sleeping upstairs in the electronic croft in Orkney can be like living in a cabin on a creaking, storm-tossed ship when the furies come calling. Step outside and you can find yourself having a surprise holiday in Bergen.

There are days when nothing moves, in or out. I've watched sophisticated visitors dance with rage at Kirkwall airport, insisting loudly that they simply have to be in London by lunch-time for an important meeting. Well, that's tough, compadres.

Urban living in the western world gives the illusion of control. Flip a switch and the light goes on. The weather can bring some inconveniences, but that's about it. Even in the small territory called Scotland, the daily consciousness of Homo Glaswegianus is radically different from that of a crofter on North Ronaldsay who has to read the weather runes.

This question about control lies at the heart of the modern project. Our leaders strut the world stage as if they were minor gods in a powerful pantheon. Backed by the unstoppable engine of modern technology, they make plans which assume the ability to manipulate events. The hubris behind this illusion of control, backed by highly developed military technology, has underwritten the Iraq adventure from the beginning. The high-tech kicking of cowed ass will sort out the dissenters, won't it? After all, every problem has a technological "fix". Mr Rumsfeld even gets a machine to sign his messages of condolence. Sincerely yours.

The explosive power of a devastating tsunami assaults not just the physical but the mental defences of a control-driven world. Doubt seeps in with the rancid sea water. This grotesque, overwhelming flood bears

133

meaning as well as bodies. It leaves soul-searching questions as well as destruction in its wake.

Was it an act of God? "Why did you do this to us, God?" cries an old woman in the Indian village of Tharangampadi, as she wades through decomposing flesh and putrid water. "What did we do to upset you? This is worse than death."

This cry has echoed down the ages, and there is no satisfactory answer to it. None. When the gods are silent, says Robert Funk, man becomes a gossip. Those theologians who simply repeat large chunks of the Bible will be compelled to fill the vacuum with stories of an intervening, angry deity who has an armoury of subtle and not so subtle weapons with which to punish the wayward. This scattergun tribal god who smashes the skulls of innocent children in order to visit the sins of the fathers and the grandfathers on them is not worthy of worship. Whatever the question is, a psychopathic control freak in the sky – one, apparently, with an abundance of socially controlling spindoctors on earth – is not the answer.

What is required in the face of this tragedy is not end-less and ultimately fruitless metaphysical speculation, but a generous global human response. The obvious immedi-ate one is that of rushing humanitarian aid to the multiple scenes of unspeakable distress. When the immediate crisis has been dealt with in the best humanly possible way, an international rebuilding programme is required.

The terrible flood pushes ever deeper questions in our direction. Can we extend this global co-operation by decisively focusing attention on the issue of world poverty? Can the divide between the rich and poor in our world go to the top of the political agenda? The Third World cops most of the catastrophes, and some of them are not unconnected to its abject poverty.

On New Year's Day, a campaign called Make Poverty History will be launched. Supported by a coalition of international aid groups, the campaign is seeking to make 2005 the year in which the world poverty agenda is decisively transformed. What the leaders are seeking goes beyond handouts for the world's poor.

"Unfair trade rules, the lack of good quality aid, and crippling debts are costing lives," says Steve Tibbett of Action Aid. "We know what the problems are but until now there has not been the political will to do something about them. We want 2005 to be remembered as the year that changed the world."

In July, Britain will host the G8 summit in Gleneagles. Representatives of the richest nations on earth will meet to discuss world problems. Can world poverty and the issues facing our fragile and vulnerable planet be addressed with seriousness? This is not a matter of quick technical "fixes" by messianic politicians, but a battle for hearts and minds that goes well beyond simply advancing western interests.

One survival of the tsunami, Pat Faragher, returned shoeless from holiday in Sri Lanka. With her husband Bill at her side, she stood at Heathrow in her socks and said: "We have lost everything – no passports, no papers, all our belongings were swept away. But we're alive." Alive, with a sense of what really matters. A stripped-down, less-cluttered sense of human identity is what we need for citizenship in the wounded global village. It should go hand in hand with an abandonment of the illusory notion of control of our world.

The Indian Ocean tragedy drives home the inter-connectedness of our world. We are our brothers and sisters keepers, and they ours. We humans have the power to visit the sins of the fathers and mothers on future generations, and it is a terrible power. The tide-borne hollow-eyed ghosts in our living rooms ask profound questions of us. And in these questions, if we have ears to hear and eyes to see, we may even get a fleeting glimpse of a transcendent stranger with nailprints in his hands.

Don't give in to the grief Fascists

Well, did you or didn't you? Did you stand to attention and observe three minutes silence for the victims of the Indian Ocean tsunami catastrophe? If you did remain silent, was it because you really wanted to do so as a respectful act of remembrance and solidarity, or was it down to social pressure? And if you didn't, do you feel guilty?

Those who read my piece last week about the Asian disaster will know that these questions aren't raised out of a lack of sympathetic awareness of the desperate nature of this devastation. My concerns have more to do with appropriate responses to tragedies, and who sets the agenda for such matters.

Some months ago I stood in silence with others on the terracing at Central Park, Cowdenbeath before kick-off time. On that occasion, the public respect was for the victims of a fire in a Glasgow store. At the time, it didn't seem so long ago since the same fans had stood to remember the two girls murdered at Soham.

I gather that the Scottish Football Association and the Scottish Football League issue guidance on such matters. Now, the SFA and the SFL can hardly organise football properly, never mind act as arbiters in matters to do with public mourning and remembrance. Yet they are regularly embroiled in debates about whether a football match should be cancelled following the death of a minor royal, or whether black armbands and a minute's silence will suffice.

What is it that links together a fire in Glasgow, the Soham murders, the death of a duchess and the Indian Ocean catastrophe? The common factor is that each event commanded the headlines for a short or a long time. In other words, the media deemed them "sexy" enough to be headed by bold black print.

What is not sexy enough is news of the thousands of deaths of malnourished children in the Third World every single day. The European Commissioners will not stand in black-suited solidarity with them. The global AIDS epidemic which is destroying whole communities will not be remembered on football terraces. The thousands killed on the roads of Britain will go unlamented, other than by their own families. There will be no roll call to mark the slaughter of the hundreds of thousands of aborted innocents in this country.

Woe betide any authority, football or otherwise, which fails to respond to the death of a royal or cultural celebrity whose death has dominated the front pages. The tabloid editors will be on their case, breathing fire as well as gin. The word "Shame!" will feature prominently on the front pages.

It was, of course, the death of Diana Princess of Wales which truly unleashed the grief fascists in all their grizzliness. The national sobalong for a populist, palpitating-lipped premier's "people's princess" became the benchmark for grief-fests. At that fevered time, anybody who failed to oblige by having a minor breakdown was regarded as seriously dysfunctional. Even that stoic institution, Caledonian MacBrayne, directed one of its ferries to stop for a minute's silence while a wreath was cast on to the waters.

There are indeed times when it is appropriate for a nation to pause and remember. I am glad to see Remembrance Day restored to its rightful place. A nation which declines to acknowledge the sacrifice of millions of its young men and women in the defence of the realm is a nation in trouble. Another great nation which refuses to allow photographs of the coffins of its own returning dead is a nation in denial. And a western coalition which declines even to count the Iraqi civilian and military dead – because they don't really "count", do they? – is also seriously deficient.

There are deaths, and deaths. Is it the numbers of the dead which justify the proliferating public remembrances? Not if they are Iraqis, or victims of poverty or AIDS or drunk drivers or a society which routinely flushes inconvenient foetuses down the pan. Is it because of the importance of the lives? I don't think so.

What I object to is being emotionally corralled and manipulated, especially by politicians and those great paragons of personal and public virtue, the saintly editors of our tabloid newspapers.

And where does this three-minutes stuff come from? Will we now have bidding remembrance wars, with the ante continually being upped? Is three minutes now the gold standard for public grief and remembrance? And who will decide whether a sad event is worth a quota of one, two, three or even five minutes? The European Fisheries Commission?

I don't object to pausing in silence for the victims of the Asian disaster; I just don't want to be hectored about it and told that three minutes is now the recommended amount. This is a time for quiet reflection; the best

139

response, though, is to give money, food, water and skills, while asking searching questions about the mass deaths of the forgotten and excluded ones of our bleeding and blessed world.

Panic on the prime minister's face

C alm down! The hyperventilation and moral panic induced by ecclesiastical interventions in the current election campaign – there is to be a general election in the next few weeks, isn't there? – is threatening to give the British body politic a heart attack. We are, says the stuttering patient with soaring blood pressure, on the verge of the kind of moral majority takeover which swept George W. Bush back into office.

Politicians can't cope when control of the national political agenda is wrested from their hands. Moral issues from "left field" bring out a cold sweat in the election managers, who hate unpredictability. Volatility in the electorate means that the political speaking-clocks who go on television to trot out the party line are thoroughly discomfited. Thank the Lord for that.

Tony Blair says that he doesn't want abortion to become an election issue. Of course he doesn't. The look of panic on the prime minister's face tells us that it is finally dawning on him that he cannot tell the punters what will, or will not be, on the political menu at election time. The delicious irony is that the very moral issues which helped the inarticulate organ-grinder get back into the presidential saddle may yet unseat the smiling-grimacing monkey. In the shadows, Count Dracula digs his opportunistic spurs into the flanks of the moral steed he hopes will carry him to unexpected victory, unaware that he cannot control his bucking bronco either.

Meanwhile, liberal commentators are in a lather of indignation. The smug holders of Britain's intellectual franchise routinely write off religious people as dim-witted God-botherers who don't even have a toe-hold on rational reality. They assume that their own elitist philosophical position does not need to be defended. They simply know. Many of them hold the electorate in utter contempt.

Anyway, it's time to slow down the breathing and swallow the beta blockers. A bit of perspective is required. To get to the heart of the matter, it's necessary to embark on a little digression.

The churches have been involved in political issues for generations. The medieval Catholic Church ran most of the caring work for Britain's ill and poor. John Knox's vision of a school in every parish was the foundation of Scotland's modern education system. Evangelical leaders like Wilberforce were at the heart of the campaign to abolish slavery. The churches were deeply involved in the civil rights movement in America, under the inspiring leadership of Martin Luther King. Rev Trevor Huddleston, Archbishop Desmond Tutu and Dr Allan Boesak were influential figures in the campaign against apartheid in South Africa.

All very inspiring, but what about the religious Right in America, where a president who executed mentally incapable prisoners when Governor of Texas and who presides over a country which allows teenagers to carry semi-automatic weapons claims the Christian moral high ground on "life" issues?

It's encouraging that there is now a growing Christian backlash in USA against their power. The hottest religious book in the USA at the moment is *God's Politics: Why the Right Gets It Wrong and the Left Doesn't Get It*, by Jim Wallis of the Sojourners' Community in Washington.

Wallis, a radical evangelical, has launched a blistering attack on fellow evangelicals who focus exclusively on abortion and homosexuality, and ignore clamant biblical issues such as war, poverty, homelessness, and generosity to the stranger. He also takes on liberals in the Democratic Party who disdainfully dismiss religious concerns as irrelevant. As his book rides high in the New York Times best-seller list and he bests the spokesmen of the religious Right on national television, Wallis's thoughtful theological critique of the Bush administration is making an impact.

So where does this leave us in today's Britain? Of course moral and spiritual issues should be on the table at election times. Yes, abortion, homosexuality and stem cell research, as well as poverty at home and abroad, good education for all, and the treatment of asylum seekers. These issues are of the very stuff of life, and voters are right to question candidates about their attitudes to these matters.

The churches have a contribution to make, but they should not be privileged over other groups. Nor should the churches pretend that they speak with one voice – after all, Wilberforce, MLK and Tutu were opposed by powerful Christian voices in their day – or that ethical issues are simple and clear-cut. Church responses to homosexuality, for instance, range all the way from Bishop Joseph Devine's shameful attack on gay teachers to the Scottish Episcopal Church's statement that living

143

in a stable same-sex relationship is not a barrier to ordination.

We live in interesting times. Let the debate about moral topics break open the bonds of sleep-inducing politics-speak. And here is one critical issue which should be at the heart of the election debate: the fitness for high office of a Christian prime minister who takes his country into a war on a false prospectus. Think about it, Tony, before you fall into a persistent legislative state from which no awakening is possible.

Crazed primates and the toothless Corgi

Antidisestablishmentarianism. It was drummed into me at school that this was the longest word in the English dictionary. I never thought I'd have the chance to use it; today, thanks to the matrimonial intentions of a dotty prince and a bidie-in who sounds like a comfortable recliner, it is one of the hottest items on the agenda of Britain's churches.

The betrothal of Prince Charming and Princess Camiknickers has got sundry Episcopal drawers in a right old twist. What fun! Rowan Williams's eyebrows have gone into overdrive as he tries to sort this one out. (At least it's a break from being beaten about the mitre by Nigerian archbishops on the subject of gay priests. When I first saw the heading "Crate of primates seized" in the Herald, I feared that more crazed archbishops were on their way to Lambeth with murderous intent, but it was only about chimpanzees. It's a funny thing, religion.)

This bizarre saga gets more preposterous by the day. The Queen has now banned the arthritic sexual athletes from spending their wedding eve in the same room. If they refuse, there could well be three people in this marriage – as Camilla might put it later – with the Queen sitting up stiffly all night between the other two. But surely this event could not unravel the Church of England's historic relationship with the state? Well, considering the relationship began with a bit of Tudor extra-mural rumpy-pumpy and was reinforced by a wee spot of execution, anything is possible.

The Roman Catholic Church must be enjoying this whole weird business. After all, the Vatican doesn't do divorce. It does annulment instead, presumably on a no-win, no-fee basis. You know, you couldn't make this stuff up. I haven't had such fun since Tom Winning did the Gay Gordons with Brian Soutar.

Ah, must be serious. The royal nuptials may yet provoke a constitutional crisis because of the knock-on effects, so to speak. Here we have a situation whereby a full Anglican wedding isn't permissible for the man who will one day be Supreme Governor of the Church of England! This is a very English unholy mess. Necessary questions about the future ecclesiastical role of a Defender of the Faith who talks to plants could lead to a further unraveling.

For instance: why should someone be Supreme Governor of the C of E simply because of who his parents are? What if the eldest son is an atheist? (It would be even more fun if Prince William announced that he was gay and wanted to become a priest, or Princess Anne sought to become a bishop.)

Is it right for the Archbishop of Canterbury to be chosen by the prime minister of the day? When Robert Runcie, a thorn in the flesh of Margaret Thatcher, retired, the two candidates produced by the nominating committee were George Carey and John Habgood, Archbishop of York. Habgood was by far the more able leader, but he was a troubler of the waters. Maggie chose the more biddable Carey-sharey man. And why should

146

the House of Commons be able to vote on the Church of England Prayer Book? Is the Beast of Bolsover a liturgical expert? It's a form of madness.

The notion of establishment goes all the way back to the Holy Roman Empire. Catholic Christianity became the official state-approved religious ideology. The Pope crowned the emperor who in turn protected the pontiff. The arrangement did provide a certain amount of stability for a while.

The establishment of the C of E is convenient in some regards. It solves the problem of who shall preside at royal marriages. In today's climate, if there were no state church, the privilege of conducting royal nuptials would go out to tender. Thus you might have the Mormons, backed by Sky Television, running the wedding of Prince William. Or you might see banners saying "Sponsored by Cowdenbeath Football Club" fluttering outside Windsor Castle.

There are two main problems with church establishment. The first is that the privileged church too easily become a toothless dog. A corgi, probably. That is why the C of E looks now looks more like a part of the heritage industry than anything else. The second problem comes when a once-strong allegiance to the state church becomes a minority sport.

The establishment of the church in Scotland is a much lighter affair. The state has no control over the Kirk. But as the national church, the Kirk has, in the past at least, been patronizing to other denominations. Now, with membership dropping, its claims to privileged status are gravely weakened. Meanwhile, this column's highly-paid moles at the Kirk's headquarters report that there is blood on the walls as yet another tedious eye-gouging, knee-in-the-groin, restructuring goes on.

Ecclesiastical privilege is past its sell-by date. So is the monarchy. I will now put on a crash helmet and prepare myself mentally for a fight against the evil forces of – all together now – antidisestablishmentarianism.

Troubling questions about the greatest show in town

J ohn Paul II's crimson-robed body lies bathed in light,
as the line of pilgrims snakes its way past the earthly
remains of the dead pontiff in St Peter's basilica. The
unprecedented number of pilgrims represents an
extraordinary outpouring of devotion for a religious
leader of global reach. Meanwhile, in other chambers,
groups of elderly men quietly and politely plot the
succession – no vulgar electioneering for them – to the
throne of Peter. It is a drama of Shakespearian
proportions.

In this column, I want to act the part of theatre
critic, both in the sense of appreciating some bits of the
action and being less than enchanted by others.

First, I need to say where I'm coming from. Before
returning to my old trade of journalism, I was an active
minister in the Church of Scotland, with radical
Presbyterianism in my soul. So you need to deduct
points for bias. I also have great admiration and affection
for Catholicism. Indeed, my most hostile mail comes
from Protestants who think I repeatedly sell the Knoxian
jersey. Quite a number of my family are Catholics. Both
in Easterhouse and as leader of the ecumenical Iona
Community, I have worked closely with Roman Catholic
priests and lay people. And I have just finished the

manuscript of a book about an entirely orthodox Catholic former tutor and mentor of mine, Father Roland Walls.

So it's not really surprising that I'm both fascinated and repelled by the greatest show in town right now. In the Herald tribute to the Pope, I expressed my admiration for the integrity and spiritual stature of John Paul. I'm not going to repeat that. What has particularly disturbed my Reformed sensibilities in the last few days has been an uncritical adulation which has bordered on the idolatrous. The industrial-strength incense which has come through the electronic ether gave me Protestant asthma.

Pope John Paul has been described as "another Christ". One person even suggested that John Paul died for our sins! For a Proddy like me, this is too much to take. And the repeated assumption that John Paul is now in heaven cannot be sustained theologically. It is an offence not only to Protestant thinking, but to good Catholic theology – yet it was put about by people who should know better. The person who stands naked before God is Karol Wojtyla, not the splendidly-robed John Paul II. The secrets of the human heart are known only to God.

The other thought which has kept coming to mind as I've viewed the images from Rome is this: where are the women? They have been reduced to the role of weeping bystanders. An all-male cast carried in the body of the pontiff. We have seen close-ups of important-looking robed males. If I were a Catholic I would be disturbed by this. It will be regarded as a sensational event if a woman is allowed to read a scripture lesson at the funeral tomorrow. I wouldn't count on it.

The plain truth is that John Paul II has reinforced all this. When the Pope arrived in America, rows of nuns

150

were paraded before him as he kissed American tarmac. A senior Sister told Denis Rice, a leading Scottish Catholic: "He got things the wrong way round: he kissed the ground and tramped on the women."

Watching the funeral tomorrow, what will it feel like to be a Catholic woman with a sense of vocation to the priesthood who has been told that she is disqualified not because of spiritual deficiencies but simply because she is a woman? This Pope has banned discussion of the subject.

What will it feel like to be a priest who, having been told that he cannot marry, has to watch while married Anglican priests who have left their church because of their opposition to the ordination of women are admitted to the Roman Catholic priesthood? And all this in a church which regards a married man – St Peter – as its first pontiff.

How will tomorrow's funeral tributes sound to an African woman dying of AIDS, knowing that her church has banned the use of condoms to prevent the spread of the HIV virus? What will be the feelings of devoted Catholic single-sex couples, who not only plead in vain for a Christian blessing, but are described as "evil"?

Or how about the mother of one of Chile's "disappeared", knowing that the Vatican secretly lobbied for General Pinochet's release from Britain?

There is a contradiction at the heart of the legend which is John Paul II. A Pope who often spoke up for the poor, and memorably rebuked George W. Bush and Tony Blair for the Iraq war adventure, had selective deafness. Priests were encouraged to get into politics in Poland as long as they supported Solidarity, but not Liberation Theology in South America. A Pope who opposed Communist tyrants and encouraged dissent in Eastern Europe strengthened the monarchical position of the papacy and clamped down on dissent in his own church. The notorious culture of secrecy has not been seriously challenged.

And it is impossible to parody the giving of a papal knighthood to Rupert Murdoch, that Dark Knight of the soul who produces "family values" newspapers like The Sun.

I have majored here on the the underbelly of John Paul II's reign, because it has been signally absent from much of the sycophantic coverage. He is a man of such stature that any reckoning of his pontificate has to be a truthful one.

John Paul II was a dedicated, gifted, charismatic, heroic man who has been the greatest religious leader of the second half of the 20th century. His standing fast against Communism has rightly made him one of the champions of the free world. And yet a fault line runs through him. Like that other rugged man of freedom, Winston Churchill, he was better at war than he was at peace. The contradictions at his core mean that he leaves both a glorious and a troublesome legacy to a probably less charismatic successor.

And so this Protestant salutes a rugged Christian soldier, a man of shining personal faith, but disembarks without apology from the adulation express. May God have mercy on the soul of his servant, Karol.

Slurry for men as grooming is booming

I look in the mirror. Hmm. A few more lines developing. In this media business, it's important to look one's best. But should the electronic crofter remortgage the croft and go for cosmetic surgery, or simply settle for the botox injections? Or will the transformation promised by the manufacturers of grossly expensive anti-ageing creams be enough?

Welcome to the age of the peacock male. According to yesterday's Herald, the health and beauty industry has increased by almost 40% over the past six years, buoyed in part by the "metrosexual man" who is leading the growth in the male grooming market.

A study by market analysts Mintel found that last year those who had been for a treatment were spending on average about £100 each. Beauty treatment for men and women in Britain last year cost a total of £1.45bn, which is more than the gross national product of some third world countries.

Women, it seems, are still much more likely than men to visit the salon, with two in five females having had a treatment in the past year. But the survey also showed that men are increasingly buying into the health and beauty sector. Actor Michael Douglas has just had his second bout of facial rehabilitation surgery; singer

Michael Jackson is basically a preposterous face-lift on spindly legs.

Orkney doesn't really do metrosexual man. I asked one crofter if he was a metrosexual and he gave me a very strange look. In common with most Orkney males, I wear a blue boiler suit and smell of slurry. The female of the species finds this irresistible – especially the animal species within three miles of the electronic croft. Once I've got my Scottish Enterprise grant, I intend to cash in on the new male beauty trend and start marketing a new aftershave lotion called "Slurry for Men".

I think we need to put this pampering into historical perspective. Take your Greeks. Your actual Greeks used to swan about naked in public baths, looking like David Beckham with a laurel wreath. Even your Platos and your Aristotles looked like models when they popped down to the neighbourhood swimming pool.

There have always been male dandies. Think of all these characters in the 17th and 18th centuries who ponced around in powdered wigs. What was all that about, for heaven's sake? Only judges and sheriffs do that now. And what about bishops in frocks, or Kirk Moderators with their lace, gaiters and buckled shoes? ("Excuse me, Mr Knox, are you a metrosexual?")

Traditionally, though, males have not been over-obsessed with hygiene and body-image. The smell wafting from the oxters of both pre- and post-neanderthal man has resembled nothing less than the stagnant breath of a constipated hedgehog. Pick up your local out-of-sorts hedgehog and you'll very quickly see what I mean. Even when deodorants first came in, bewildered men who had received them as presents sprayed them on to their tweed jackets. It is evidence of the sheer power of the mating instinct that such men were often married.

Ah, but now it's so different. Grooming is booming. Men have baths and showers. They even wash their hair. They spend money themselves on deodorants and moisturisers. They work out in the gym to get rid of unsightly beer bellies. Belching and farting are no longer essential parts of the male repertoire. What a revolution!

While three-and-a-half years ago just 25% of male skincare products were purchased by men, today the level is 40%, according to Boots sales data. Increasingly, men are selecting products for themselves, rather than relying on partners to buy for them.

One thing I definitely draw the line at is having my body hair plucked out. There was a photograph in the papers the other day of the Chelsea football team minus their shirts. Not a body hair was to be seen. That's today's fashion. Young men go into salons to have their hairy chests waxed clean.

Confession time: underneath the electronic crofter's boiler suit there is a very hairy body. I have in my time been cruelly compared to a gorilla. When I slouch the beaches of Orkney, children – and even adults – run away screaming. Mind you, you need fur when you swim in the northern isles. On one occasion I was taken into captivity and only released when the electronic crofterina signed for me. Sometimes it's hard to be a man.

No way will I subject myself to having boiling wax poured over my magnificent physique and having the hair wheeched out. You would hear the screams in Shetland. No, not even if I'm selected to play for Cowdenbeath again, and we're asked to take part in a photo-shoot for Hello magazine.

But here are some final thoughts for you. When was it that image became more important than character in our society? When was it that ageing became a sin? Is cool, sweat-free Narcissus really the icon that modern men should aspire to?

And don't forget – soon to be showing at a store near you: new male grooming products from the global brand name, House of Slurry. Buy while stocks last. You know it makes sense.